How To Be First In A Second Marriage

Rose Sweet

How To Be First In A Second Marriage

COLLEGE PRESS
PUBLISHING COMPANY
Joplin, Missouri

Cover Design by Mark A. Cole

The Steps to Emotional Freedom, the Love Questions and the Royal
Promises have been modified and expanded with permission and are
based on those taught by Dr. Gary Lawrence in his University for
Successful Living seminars

International Standard Book Number 0-89900-818-6

Table of Contents

WHO NEEDS THIS BOOK?

Let's face it, we all want to be first in *any* marriage. Men want to be king of the castle and women want to be . . . well, if you are like me, we usually want to be "Queen of Everything"!

Unfortunately too many other things occupy the honored throne that should be reserved for each other in marriage. In this book we focus on how ex-spouses and stepchildren can become a priority over new spouses, but there are many other people and things that *keep us from being first* in our marriages:

Does your spouse's career seem to always come first?

Are you tired of playing second-fiddle to the kids?

Is a meddling mother-in-law taking over your marriage?

If so, **this book is for you.** In Parts I and II (*The Dungeon* and *The Castle Walls*), we'll show you exactly how to unplug from those people, places or things that prevent spouses from making each other first in their marriage. If you don't think you have any trouble with priorities, then Part III (*The Royal Treatment*) is loaded with new principles and practices to help any couple build their marriage, first or second, into the rich and deeply satisfying union God intended for us.

Whether you are in a first or second marriage, healing from a divorce or soon to be remarried, we know you'll find *hope, help and healing* between the pages of *How to Be First in a Second Marriage*!

Introduction

very failed marriage deserves to be put out of its misery, buried and properly grieved.

THE PLIGHT OF THE NEW WIFE

We rarely hear about the troubles, hurts and anxieties suffered by the new wife in her husband's second marriage. She may be a good Christian woman: someone's sister, daughter, friend. She fell in love with and married a man who failed in his first marriage. She's chosen to dedicate her life and love to him, and is trying to follow her heart in being the best wife she can be. If this is her first marriage, she brings all the hopes and dreams any woman brings to her new life. Maybe it's her second marriage, and she's determined this time to make it work. She hopes to be a good stepmom, eager to love her husband's children. However, these lofty goals don't always work out, especially without a clear understanding of the dynamics of blended families.

Sometimes society tends to overglorify biological parenthood. Unfortunately the miracle of birth does not automatically

Introduction

equip a person to be a good parent, nor does it qualify one for sainthood. Stepparents can and do play a vital and crucial role in the loving, nurturing and raising of children.

THE NEW ROLE OF THE EX-SPOUSE

Ex-spouses may, understandably, have trouble adjusting to the end of a dream, coping with the former mate's new marriage and creating a new and different life for themselves.

While the role with the children obviously continues, the relationship to the ex-spouse is altered drastically. Consciously or not, the ex-spouse may have trouble reacting in a rational manner. But even for him or her, healing and new beginnings *are* within reach.

THE EMOTIONAL BONDAGE OF THE SECOND-TIME SPOUSE

If a man's home is his castle, why are so many men living in the dungeon of bondage to their old relationships? Understanding the chains of emotional bondage that tie them to their ex-spouses is the first necessary step in breaking those chains. No new marriage is capable of reaching the depths of love and satisfaction we long for until the ties binding men to the old marriage are broken. Husbands and their new wives now have a practical plan for clearly defining the boundaries and roles of their new marriage. *How to Be First in a Second Marriage* explains how to break those ties and explores the fears and challenges facing the husband and the new wife, as well as providing advice which can apply to ex-wives, ex-husbands, new husbands — even grandparents and other interested parties. It clearly defines the boundaries and roles of the new marriage and offers a successful plan for making it work.

Part I

The Dungeon

"What other Dungeon is so dark as one's own heart!
What jailer so inexorable as one's self!"

Nathaniel Hawthorne - 1851
The House of the Seven Gables

Chapter 1

You Might Have a Problem If . . .

ane sent the kids to her sister's for the evening. As she and her husband, Tim, were sitting down to a romantic candlelight dinner together, he remembered it was the first of the month and the child support check to his ex-wife was due. "Jane, honey," said Tim, "I need to run this check over to Ann's house and I'll be right back. Okay?"

Jane pleaded in her most convincing tone, "Tim, do you have to go tonight? Do you have to go right this minute?"

Tim pecked her on the cheek as he grabbed his keys and went out the door. "Honey, she needs the money and I want to abide by the court agreement about timely child support payments. I promise I'll be back in just ten minutes!"

Jane forced a half-smile and blew out the candles as he left. As angry thoughts raced through her mind, she began to chide herself for feeling so insecure. Tim was being honorable by getting the money to his ex-wife on time, so she felt guilty about being angry. *He will be right back, he promised, and he's married to ME. He loves ME. I'm being so stupid!* Jane continued to obsess.

Over an hour later Tim arrived home to a cold dinner and a cold wife. Jane's attitude fluctuated back and forth from

The Dungeon

acceptance to anger. Right now she was angry. Tim cuddled her and apologized for being late, saying Ann had needed to talk about the kid's school problems. As he kissed her neck gently, Jane felt angry-guilty-angry-guilty as Tim led her into the bedroom. They made love that night, but Jane stuffed her still hurt feelings inside as she drifted off to a restless sleep.

Jane's feelings were normal responses to rejection. In defense of themselves, many husbands claim "doing their duty" as an excuse when their current wife or family are put on hold or put in second place to the ex-wife. It's time to stop looking at the surface *actions* and start examining the subsurface *attitudes*. What could Tim have done differently?

While you wives probably have a good idea, husbands might need to reexamine the options:

Mail the check ahead of time. If Tim wanted to be honorable he shouldn't have waited until the last minute.

The husband should call the "ex" and seek forgiveness for not having the money to her sooner. Tell her he'll be by first thing tomorrow.

Honor the commitment. If Tim did drive over, he should've honored his ten-minute commitment to Jane, made an appointment for the next day to talk on the phone about the kids' school problems, and politely but firmly excused himself.

Prearrange a set time each week on the phone to review the kids' welfare, school, etc. While kids' crises can't be scheduled, husbands should learn the difference between an emergency and a situation which can be talked about the next morning or at some later time.

Tim put Jane and her planned evening and her emotional needs behind the ex-wife's needs and behind his own needs to feel responsible. But Tim probably doesn't see it that way. Tim thinks his wife is jealous and insecure, and the problem is hers. Men like Tim often rationalize they are also taking care of their children's needs by personally delivering the check on time.

Instead of responding on an emotional level, Tim should have stopped and reviewed the facts. The kids' immediate needs are the roof over their head, the food on the table and knowing that both Mom and Dad, wherever they live, love them forever. Those needs were already met that night. There was nothing so urgent that Tim should have left Jane in the middle of their evening together. Unless there is some physical or emotional emergency with the children, the new wife's needs should always come first.

Tim's chains of emotional bondage are residual feelings of *failure* in the marriage to Ann, and *guilt* for abandoning his kids. To escape the pain of his emotions, Tim tries to "make up" for the past by always taking good care of Ann and the kids. When he performs as their continuing caretaker, Tim's guilt is soothed by feeling he's done a good job.

Jane is also in emotional bondage to her husband, Tim. Jane needs to speak up and lovingly advise or remind Tim of his options. Sometimes husbands react from old habits without stopping to think. Jane also should not bury her normal feelings of anger at rejection, as they will surely grow into bitterness. Like so many wives, Jane's chains are her fear of conflict or rejection by Tim. If Jane feels insecure, Tim should help to meet her emotional needs.

Are you in emotional bondage to *your* new spouse?

SIGNS OF TROUBLE

I sure didn't smell trouble brewing in my new marriage. I was in love and still optimistic that this time around everything would be okay. Unfortunately a whole different set of problems was simmering and was soon to boil over! Check this list to see if you recognize any of the telltale signs of potential problems in your new marriage. (Keep in mind that these are guidelines. The roles may be switched around in various configurations depending on the parameters of a given marriage/divorce situation.):

The Husband

The husband's priority is keeping his ex-wife "happy."

The Dungeon

He still helps her with her car problems.

He still owns a business or has other financial holdings with his ex-wife.

He keeps her name on his credit accounts to "help her out."

He keeps pictures or other mementos of his ex-wife.

He tells the new wife she's jealous and to get over it.

He prioritizes the ex-wife's requests over the new wife's.

He tells the new wife she shouldn't feel insecure.

He talks to the ex-wife about their kids, but excludes his new wife from giving input.

He meets with the ex-wife to "go over things" but never tells his new wife.

He frequently spends time in phone conversations with his ex-wife.

He chooses his children's "side" over the new wife's.

He doesn't allow his new wife to discipline his children when appropriate.

He avoids dealing with the new wife and makes no attempt at establishing a working relationship.

The New Wife

The new wife worries that the husband is still emotionally tied to the ex-wife.

She compares her figure, cooking or talents to the ex-wife's.

She frequently seeks reassurance of being better than the ex-wife.

She competes with or feels like a loser around the ex-wife.

She feels angry when the ex-wife calls.

She fears the ex-wife still wields some control over her new husband.

She is excluded from parenting functions regarding her stepchildren.

She is not given authority by her husband to discipline her stepchildren.

She avoids the new wife.

She becomes friends with the ex-wife and compares notes about the husband.

She's hurt or angry that the stepchildren reject her.

The Ex-Wife

The ex-wife calls several times a day or late in the evening.

She is intimate or flirts with her ex-husband in front of his new wife.

She deliberately snubs or excludes the new wife from conversation.

She asks her ex-husband to do little favors around her house, and he does.

She is late picking up or dropping off the kids.

She belittles her ex-husband or his new wife to her children.

She calls her ex-husband when she needs advice on something.

She threatens to withhold visitation as a punishment or to get her way.

She threatens court action to get her way.

She tells the new wife private details about the first marriage.

She invites herself to all the family gatherings and social functions.

She commits the children to social obligations or other events on the ex-husband's visitation time without checking with him first.

Do any of these sound familiar? These potentially unhealthy situations happen all the time and you may hardly notice they exist. Oftentimes remarried people notice only their uneasy, uncomfortable or unhappy feelings after the situations arise.

Jack Kent wrote a "Little Golden Book" for families in various forms of denial called, *There's No Such Thing as a Dragon* (Racine, WI: Western Publishing Co., 1975). It's a story about a young boy who notices a baby dragon romping through the living room. As he tries to alert the family members to the fact "there's a dragon in the house," no one wants to admit there's a problem, no one wants to deal with the problem, and if there was a problem, it's so small they don't need to worry about it. With time, the dragon grows and grows, until his head is

The Dungeon

sticking out the second story window and his body fills the first floor. Even then, family members are still walking *around* him. Finally, when the house is bursting at the beams, Mom and Dad acknowledge the dragon's existence. Immediately, the dragon (problem) begins to shrink.

Similarly, before a doctor removes a tumor, he conducts certain tests to determine how it got there in the first place, and treats the root cause. After the growth is removed, the patient usually continues on medication, and must make permanent changes in his life to ensure against recurrence. Merely cutting the growth out will not guarantee the disease won't resurface. Despite the urge for a "quick fix" excision of the ex-spouse from *your* life, the real problem will not end and will actually make matters worse if we don't identify the *root problems*.

The next chapters will identify the root causes of problems in a second marriage.

Chapter 2

Buried Alive

When I was dating my soon-to-be husband, I met and fell in love with his two-year-old, curly blonde-haired son, a spunky spittin' image of his handsome Dad. In love and excited about a new marriage, I couldn't wait to be a stepmother and looked forward to establishing a friendly relationship with the ex-wife, whom I hadn't yet met. I knew we could all be adults about the whole thing, that we'd all be on civil terms. I even thought of some exchanges to break the ice with her. Unfortunately, I soon found out the only thing she wanted to exchange was a cold, icy stare. The first time we met she grabbed her son close to her, gave me a long, hard glare and turned her back on me without a word.

In my naivete, I assumed I could get her to like me eventually. I wanted so much to create the happy family situation of which I'd always dreamed, and I thought it would be no problem to include an ex-wife. I was so focused on fixing my relationship with her, I hardly noticed the way my husband still responded to her. He was loaded down with unresolved feelings of failure and guilt, still in emotional bondage to his ex-wife. As he apparently had done in their marriage, he'd let her dictate his actions, and he continued to do so in *our* marriage.

The Dungeon

Was I confused! Their divorce was long over, and now we were married. He was living with, sleeping with and loving *me*. Why was *she* still such a powerful influence over him? The problems began to get bigger, and the next few years of our new marriage were spent like all new marriages, sorting through the emotional baggage we each brought to the union. I knew second marriages had some "excess baggage" like ex-spouses and stepkids, but the little carry-on bag I thought I'd be dealing with turned out to be a giant steamer trunk!

WHEN THE FIRST MARRIAGE IS STILL ALIVE

How about those scary movies we see these days? It's almost the end of the movie, the hero has beaten the dickens out of the bad guy, and his battered body lies still in the lower corner of the movie screen, just behind the now-embracing hero and heroine. All too often, the bad guy just isn't dead yet! I remember, long before today's common grisly horror movies, watching *Wait Until Dark*. As I was relishing a happy ending, the bad guy, still alive, suddenly leapt out on the giant screen at Audrey Hepburn. In unison, the whole theater of movie-goers screamed and jumped out of their seats.

Divorce is frequently just like those movies. The pain and frustration of a failed marriage wears us down to the point that all we want to do is escape the pain and file for divorce. Once the judge signs the papers, we breathe a sigh of relief and, after a period, we resume our lives, often in a new relationship. It's just a matter of time, though, before we realize all we did was *bury the old marriage alive*. The same conflicts we experienced in the old marriage are still there. The same habitual attitudes and responses that we struggled with in the old marriage often still prevail when we're dealing with an "ex."

That's what happened to my husband, and as I soon realized, had been happening to all my divorced friends. Try as they might to be friends with their ex-spouses, the friendships were generally surface behavior. There were still varying levels of tension, battles for control, anger, jealousy, distrust and a myriad of other negative emotional response patterns. The relationships really hadn't ended. The circumstances had changed, but the relationship was still alive; the old dance tunes were still playing.

Most people can relate to this phenomenon in another way by analyzing their relationship with a parent. You likely know someone in your family or circle of friends who grew up, moved out of the house, got married, lives in another state, but is still emotionally controlled by mom or dad. It seems they still have a 1,000 mile long umbilical cord! Unless we learn to break the mental and emotional ties with our ex-spouse, the old "marriage" will still be alive. Many people seek counseling during the last part of their marriages in an effort to salvage the relationship. Unfortunately, most do not continue counseling *after* the divorce to learn how to put the marriage to a final death. **Every failed marriage deserves to be put out of its misery, buried and properly grieved.**

Chained in the Dungeon of Mental and Emotional Bondage

If a man's home is his castle, why are so many men living in the dungeon of bondage to their old relationships? Let's take this medieval musing one step further:

Most people in second marriages still live in the dungeon of emotional bondage to the people and circumstances of the first marriage.

The bad news is our new marriage will never be able to reach the deep levels of love and satisfaction we dream of unless the chains of bondage to the old marriage are broken.

A new marriage can't thrive while the old one's alive.

The Escape Plan

Escaping the dungeon begins with going back to the old marriage and beginning the final execution process. We'll BURY the old relationship, COMPLETE the grieving process,

The Dungeon

set new BOUNDARIES to keep the family safe, and BUILD the marriage on new principles, priorities and practices. Ready? Let the execution begin!

> *"For I know the plans I have for you," declares the Lord,*
> *"plans to prosper you and not to harm you,*
> *plans to give you hope and a future."*
> *Jeremiah 29:11*

Chapter 3

Bitterness
The First Chain of Mental
and Emotional Bondage

✠

"Each heart knows its own bitterness . . ." Proverbs 14:10

hortly after we were married, my husband and I
went to counseling. We wanted to learn how to deal
with our growing problems that seemed to center
around lack of boundaries between old and new marriages.
We ended up in Phoenix, Arizona at the New Life Dynamics
Christian Counseling Center. The founder, Dr. Gary Lawrence,
bases his teachings on Scripture, and particularly emphasizes
the adverse effects on our lives of "the root of bitterness."

"Most counseling today is nothing more than Band-Aid®
therapy," notes Dr. Lawrence (*Rejection Junkies*, [self-published,
1996]). The counseling staff at New Life Dynamics acknowl-
edges some of the popular behavior modification techniques
as helpful tools, but cautions they are only temporary balm to
our emotions. The staff teaches that unless the root cause of
mental and emotional conflict is "identified, isolated and elimi-
nated," emotional problems *will* continue. *This root cause is bitterness in one or more of its many forms.*

Dr. Lawrence patiently listened to our stories and gave us
his diagnosis. "The problem is not the ex-wife," he explained.
"The problem is your attitude toward her. Now listen to me.

The Dungeon

Yeah, she's pulled some rotten stuff. She's being unfair, and I agree she's treated you terribly. But those are *her* problems. Your problem is that you are bitter toward her and need to take responsibility for your own attitude. You're locked in a negative pattern of responding to her rejection of you. As a matter of fact, you're both 'Rejection Junkies'!"

"What is this guy *talking* about?" I thought to myself as Dr. Lawrence told my husband and I that we were bitter. We'd just complained of the problems we'd been having with the ex-wife, and this guy tells us the problem is us! I wasn't bitter. *Thin-lipped, sour-pussed angry people are bitter, but not me,* I thought.

THE REJECTION CONNECTION

As we continued the counseling, his message became clear. From the time we are young, people reject us in many ways. We learn to automatically respond to rejection early in life, either by withdrawing, attacking, becoming anxious, having wounded spirits, or developing a sense of guilt, loss, fear or abandonment. *These responses are all forms of bitterness!*

We carry these response patterns into every relationship in our lives, where they always cause conflict. We brought them into our first marriage and they're in our current marriage. Every day people reject us. Every day we automatically respond with various forms of bitterness. Our reaction to the rejection keeps us connected to those who reject us, hence we form a Rejection Connection.

Some say the strongest human desire is for love. While there are many definitions of "love," they are all various forms of acceptance. *Humans' deepest motivations are to gain acceptance (love) and avoid rejection.*

Remember the first married couple, Adam and Eve? Their actions were rejected by God, and ever since, humankind has had a strong desire to regain acceptance, to belong.

When we're separated from God, we begin to look for ways to get the "feeling" of being loved and accepted by others, seemingly blind to the fact that others will NEVER satisfy like God will.

Neil T. Anderson writes in *Victory over the Darkness* (Ventura, CA: Gospel Light, 1990) about the three basic and continuous emotional needs in our lives which started with Adam and Eve:

Acceptance was replaced by rejection, therefore we have a need to belong. Adam fully "belonged" to God and to all things in the garden, before he alienated himself. Even God saw that it was not good that Adam was "alone" and to complete his sense of belonging, gave him Eve. *Because of rejection we fear abandonment.*

Innocence was replaced by guilt and shame, therefore we need to restore our feelings of self-worth. Adam and Eve didn't exactly have the highest levels of self-esteem after their sin. Our response to rejection is often to seek to restore our own feelings of self-worth. *Because of rejection we fear loss of self.*

Authority was replaced by weakness and helplessness, therefore we have a need for strength and self-control. Adam was in control, feeling confident and secure in his God-given authority before the fall. Our response to rejection causes us to seek to regain that sense of self-control. *Because of rejection we fear being dominated.*

In any marriage we constantly try to secure our sense of belonging, of feeling good about ourselves and of being in control. When we don't get satisfaction, we react in "bitterness." Tragically, *bitterness fixates us at the point of our pain!*

In Divorce, the Rejection Never Ends

There are many ways rejection continues *after* the divorce. The ex-spouse talks down about the other parent to the children, extended family, friends or business acquaintances. An ex-spouse continues to exclude the other parent or stepparent from the children's lives. The children choose one parent over the other, or resent one parent for what they did to the other parent. The new spouse takes a parent's place with the children. The children decide they want to live with the other parent. The ex-spouse tries to sabotage the other parent's new

The Dungeon

marriage. The list goes on, even when the children are grown. Who will walk the bride down the aisle? Who will be invited to the wedding and who will be asked to stay home? When the grandchildren come, will they love Grandma or Grandpa better? Will the family visit Mom this year, or Dad?

If we don't learn to change our reaction to the rejection, we're doomed to a long life of mental and emotional conflict and increasing bitterness.

Rejection will continue until the day we die, but we no longer have to react to rejection with bitterness.

> *"Get rid of all bitterness, rage and anger."*
> *Ephesians 4:31a*

Chapter 4

Guilt
The Second Chain of Mental and Emotional Bondage

"*Then I acknowledged my sin to you . . .
and you forgave the guilt of my sin.*"
Psalm 32:5

At dinner in a restaurant one night, my four-year-old-stepson announced: "My mom hates you!" Well, the noodles about half-caught in my throat as I forced a smile and replied, "Gee, that's too bad, honey." I paused. " I don't hate her, and I hope someday she and I will be friends." I looked over at my husband who was, in his usual fashion, wishing someone would change the subject . . . fast.

My stepson seemed satisfied with my reply, and went on to discuss the Ninja Turtles. Although I didn't realize it at the time, his comment had stirred up fears of rejection in me. I feared his mother's rejection because then people might say I wasn't a good new wife or stepmother if we didn't get along. I was under the false illusion that I could actually control whether we had a friendship or not! I thought it was *all up to me* and that I just had to work a littler harder, or try another way to make her my friend. Then we'd all be happy. I was also worried if she didn't like me, she'd turn her son against me.

The Dungeon

Unable to have children of my own, I didn't want to lose his love.

I feared my husband's rejection because I knew he also expected me to get along with her. If I made waves with her, we'd both pay the price. I was surprised but happy to find out later in counseling that my guilt feelings had been nothing more than "false guilt."

THE DIFFERENCE BETWEEN FALSE AND GENUINE GUILT

Just what is false guilt? It's just another form of bitterness. In his book, *Rejection Junkies*, Dr. Lawrence gives these definitions:

False Guilt - An anxiety created from a fear of being rejected for lack of performance.

Genuine Guilt - A grieving created by the Holy Spirit over a situation.

With genuine guilt, you KNOW you have something to grieve about. With false guilt, you FEEL you have something to be ashamed about. When we're in emotional bondage, there's conflict between *what we know* and *how we feel*.

I hadn't said or done anything to intentionally harm my husband's ex-wife. I had always tried to be friendly and kind to her. But because all my life I'd tried to gain acceptance and avoid rejection from others, I feared future rejection if I didn't "perform" by making the friendship happen, and I "felt" guilty.

Why? I lacked a sense of my true identity, and relied on what other people thought of me to validate my self-worth. On the surface I knew I was intelligent, educated, fun-loving and good at my job, but I didn't feel I was good enough unless we were all getting along and I was keeping the peace. In this case, I'd plugged my self-worth into the opinions of three people whom I'd really only known a short time. I was in emotional bondage to my husband, his ex-wife and my stepson!

Are you or your spouse connected to others through false guilt?

"See . . . your guilt is taken away and your sin atoned for."
Isaiah 6:7b

Chapter 5

Fear
The Third Chain of Mental and Emotional Bondage

✠

ill listened grimly as his attorney told him, "Technically, you have 50/50 rights in decisions about the health, education and welfare of your son — but in practice, Bill, the parent with physical custody calls the shots. You have just about as much power in parenting your son as a visiting uncle."

When Bill's ex-wife had gotten angry in the past, she'd threatened, "Believe me, our days in this town are numbered!" Lacking primary custody, many fathers, like Bill, fear that their ex-wives, if angered, will deprive them of visitation, or worse, will move the children out of state or to another distant location where visits would be costly and infrequent.

Many husbands who are angry at their ex-wives will behave politely or even intimately with them in person or on the phone, not wanting to make waves or show their anger and frustration. Interviews with these men reveal that the motive for their seemingly two-faced behavior is fear. Caught in the middle, these men could be called "emotional bigamists."

Many ex-wives use this threat as a power play when things do not go their way. Fathers today have little confidence in the courts' protecting their parental rights.

The Dungeon

Being a noncustodial father is tragic for a man who loves his children. Despite the bad rap deadbeat dads give divorced fathers, my husband, like so many others, always pays his child support, attends school functions, involves himself in his son's sports and yearns to have his son in his own home. Some seem to forget it's not just a mother's arms that ache to hold their child or to tuck them safely into bed every night.

Ex-husbands' fears, like all fears, are various types of the same thing: rejection. Rejection can take many forms, either overt or covert. If we're afraid of rejection, we'll stay in bondage to that person, place or circumstance that might reject us.

> *Fear of rejection (abandonment) is based*
> *on our first emotional need — to belong.*

LARRY'S FEAR OF FAILURE

Larry had been a good financial provider in his first marriage. His wife hadn't worked, and he enjoyed a successful career. Larry, a hard-driving businessman, had never perceived himself as a failure. When his marriage ended in divorce, he continued to take care of his ex-wife's needs and overcompensated for all the children's needs and wants. He didn't feel like a failure as long as he remained the financial caretaker.

Larry eventually remarried and started a second family. His ex-wife never remarried and continued to enjoy Larry's active presence in, and full financial support of her family. In addition to paying hefty child support and alimony, he took care of her car, her lawn and did her taxes each year. He bought the kids everything and anything they wanted, and gave in to their frequent whining and self-centered whims.

When he remarried, the time he spent doing things for his ex-wife did not endear him to his new bride. Although Larry had legally ended the marriage and was no longer "in love" with his ex-wife, he was still emotionally married to her. Larry couldn't face the feeling that he'd failed as a husband and father, and kept working hard through his second marriage to avoid repeating such feelings. Larry's fear of failure kept him in emotional bondage to his ex-wife and children.

> *Fear of failure is based on our second*
> *emotional need — a sense of self-worth.*

FEAR OF LACK OF CONTROL

When a parent thinks an ex-spouse may take the children and run, he/she feels powerless and out of control. The common response, to placate him/her and not risk his/her anger, is *an attempt to maintain control of the situation*. Later (chapter eighteen) we'll touch on the basic human temperaments and learn how even the most meek and mild-mannered of us have developed ways to be "in control."

> *Fear of loss of control is based*
> *on our third emotional need — security.*

FEAR IS A LACK OF FAITH

Neil Anderson states it quite simply in *Victory over the Darkness*: "If fear is controlling your life, then faith is not." We can't avoid our relationship with God in all this. The reason we have so many mental and emotional problems in our marriages and our lives, is that our souls are at war with our spirits.

Our soul (mind, emotions and will) keeps trying to meet our emotional needs (to belong, to have self-worth, to be in control) through others, when we can only really have our needs permanently met through our relationship with God. When we have the Spirit of God in us, we have all we need, yet we continue to look to the world.

This is not to say we don't still need people. We do. God gave us each other to love and be loved. However, we do need to get over our fear of failure, rejection and loss of control. That can only come when we fully realize how wonderful, special and precious we are to God, even when we fail Him,

The Dungeon

ourselves or others. We're accepted and loved by God even when people reject us. *Freedom from fear comes with the understanding of our true identity as a precious child of God.*

> *"But perfect love drives out fear . . . ."*
> *1 John 4:18*

Chapter 6

Common Fears

❖

*"You will keep in perfect peace him whose mind is steadfast,
because he trusts in you."*
Isaiah 26:3

Chris was 35 and had been married to Linda for six years. They had two children, but divorced shortly after the second child was born. Linda never remarried and had custody of the two children. Now Chris was newly remarried to Gina and the proud father of a new baby boy!

Chris had grown up in a large family with lots of aunts, uncles and cousins. His mother and father had decided to host a family reunion and were expecting over 100 guests for the occasion at their lakeside home. Although she was eager to show off the new baby, Chris's new wife, Gina, was less than thrilled.

"Your Mom actually invited your ex-wife to your family reunion! She hasn't been part of your family for years!" Gina had never felt comfortable with Chris's ex-wife, Linda. Unfortunately Linda remained contemptuous of her ex-husband and never missed an opportunity to shame or humilate him to her children. She was also jealous of and resented Gina's influence as stepmother to her kids. Every time they were together, Linda

The Dungeon

said hurtful things to Gina, yet purred seductively to Chris as if they were still married.

Linda had also tried, through gossip and letters, to sabotage Gina's new relationship with her mother-in-law. Gina had replaced Linda not only in the marriage to Chris, but in the rest of the extended family. Losing status as "family" was something Linda would not accept.

Although Chris's mother knew of the strained relationship, she felt sorry for Linda who'd never remarried, and whom she knew missed being part of the family. "Linda is still mother to my grandchildren, and I consider her family too. I haven't seen her in a long time. Just because you divorced her doesn't mean I have to!" she told Chris when he asked her why she'd invited his ex-wife to the reunion.

"Mom, out of consideration for my new wife and the scenes that invariably happen every time Linda's around us, I'd like you to take her off the guest list. We're bringing the new baby, and I don't want anything to ruin Gina's evening of showing off our son to the family. I want to introduce my new wife to the whole family without my ex-wife hanging around."

He then suggested to his mother, "If you want to spend some time with Linda and the kids, why don't the two of you go to lunch sometime, or take the kids to the park?"

Chris's mother was shocked. "What's wrong with you? Can't you let go of the past? I just don't understand why you feel uncomfortable around Linda. After all, she's the mother of your children! Your father isn't going to be pleased with your attitude. Your brother certainly never makes waves like you do. Why can't you and Gina just put your personal feelings aside for one day?"

Chris had been firmly headed in the right direction, but as soon as Mom accused him of not being able to let go of the past, he began to doubt himself (false guilt). Her suggestion that Dad might reject him hit a nerve too. And there was also that age old comparison to his "perfect" big brother. "Okay, Mom, you win." Chris, the "Rejection Junkie," had just given in to the big fix.

At the reunion Linda showed up in something black and revealing, draping herself over Chris throughout the evening. "I hope it won't take you too long to get that weight off after the baby," she cooed to Gina, feigning concern about how the baby *did* look a little jaundiced. Of course neither Gina nor Chris wanted to start trouble at the party, so they put on their phony smiles and masked their anger, hurt and frustration. Gina got a headache and Chris ended up drinking a little too much that night.

Chris was in bondage to his mother, father, brother, ex-wife and new wife. He didn't want their rejection. He didn't want to "fail" Dad. He was in bondage to his ex-wife because he was reluctant to set or enforce a boundary with her, fearing her anger and possible retaliation through his family or the children. Chris was also bitter toward his wife, whom he felt had pressured him to make a stand in the first place. Poor guy. What a waste of a good party!

Chris had a number of options, including leaving the reunion early or not attending at all. However, as long as he remained in fear of what others would think if he left early or didn't show up, he also remained in bondage. What do you think Chris should have done?

MEN IN THE MIDDLE

Almost 50% of divorced men remarry within one year of the divorce. Many remarried men feel like they have two "wives." They may spend a lot of energy trying to keep the ex-wife happy, fearful of further rejection, revenge or retaliation.

The new wife places normal demands on her husband's time and energy, but he may also have to deal with problems that stem from her own fears, insecurity or jealousy. He may have to explain why he paid his ex-wife's alimony but not the new wife's car payment. When he makes decisions to keep the ex-wife satisfied, he may be sacrificing time, attention or energy with his new wife. The poor guy feels like he's being pulled from both sides. The sad fact is, the new wife takes the brunt of his frustration.

The Dungeon

Unfortunately, most husbands are in some form of emotional bondage to their ex-wives and children out of unresolved feelings of failure, guilt (both genuine and false) and fear. They bend over backwards for their "ex," or overcompensate with the children, all in an effort to pay for their "sin" of divorce.

WHAT'S HE AFRAID OF?

When new wives become aware of what is really motivating their husbands' behavior, they can begin to take things less personally. They fear all types of rejection and failure, which leads to feelings of loss of self-worth and control. Common fears include:

Fear of failing (again) as a husband.
Fear of failing (again) as a father.
Fear of losing his children.
Fear of losing his children's love.
Fear that the courts will believe the ex-wife's lies.
Fear of ongoing rejection by the woman he once loved.
Fear of ongoing rejection by family or ex-family.
Fear of being reminded how he failed.
Fear of his children loving their mother more than they love him.
Fear that he shouldn't have married his new wife. Most men won't share this fear with their new wives, but the thought invariably comes into their minds, especially after their first big fight, "Did I make a big mistake?"
Fear that if the second marriage fails, he'll be alone again. Many men won't burn their bridges, "just in case."

THE EX-WIFE'S FEARS

When David and Leslie returned from their Caribbean honeymoon cruise, their answering machine held three nasty messages from David's ex-wife, Nina.

A year ago Nina had seemed to accept the fact that her ex-spouse was dating and had become serious about Leslie. She had also seemed reasonably calm when they'd announced their engagement and set a wedding date. Both David and Leslie were grateful that Nina appeared to be taking things so well. No one realized the effect their actual wedding ceremony would have on Nina.

What was the problem? Reality had set in. Although we often plan for how we'll handle a traumatic event, our responses when such events actually occur are often unpredictable.

The ex-wife is often just as eager as her ex-husband to ease the hurt of divorce and return to a "normal" life as quickly as possible. They color their hair, shop for new clothes or lose ten pounds. Eventually the pain dulls and they celebrate "getting over" their husbands. In reality those feelings are buried just beneath the surface.

When events such as his remarriage or the birth of his and his new wife's new baby occur, strong reactions result from pent-up bitterness, especially if she hasn't remarried. The husband, the new wife and the ex-wife benefit from understanding and preparing for such reactions.

Ex-wives have lost their husbands, their dreams, and often suffer the continued insult of late support checks, broken promises and no-show visitations.

Ex-wives may also fear that the ex-husband has forgotten their love or no longer harbors *any* positive feelings toward her at all. She also fears that the new wife will take her place in her children's hearts. Reassurances and positive actions can help ease the latter fear.

COMMON FEARS OF NEW WIVES

Women may compare themselves to "the other woman" because they think *he* compares. New wives need to remember they are usually not only in emotional bondage to the ex-wife (the object of their fear) but to their new husbands, whose rejection they fear. Some of the most common fears which keep the new wife chained in mental and emotional bondage are:

The Dungeon

Fear of the ex-wife controlling his actions.
Fear of him taking the ex-wife's side over hers.
Fear of financial trouble (child support or alimony payments).
Fear of his old sentimental or romantic feelings for his ex-wife.
Fear of his siding with his children.
Fear of rejection by his children.
Fear of rejection by his family.
Fear of him divorcing her. Remarried couples always struggle
   with some level of insecurity knowing at least one of them
   broke a lifetime vow and may do it again.

New wives usually step into a ready-made family and have to
figure out how to fit in. The empty space has another woman's
size and shape, and the kids already have a mother. Rather
than try to fill that hole, new wives can learn to bring a whole
new special presence to the family. The old family can be dou-
bly blessed with the new wife's own unique gifts, talents and
love for all the family members, even his ex-wife!

> *"Consider the blameless, observe the upright;*
> *there is a future for the man of peace."*
> *Psalm 37:37*

Chapter 7

Stop, Thief!

emember the definition of "bitterness?" Ask yourself what people or circumstances cause you to have these emotional responses:

An inward resentment

A wounded spirit

A guilt

A fear

An anxiety

An avoidance

A sense of abandonment

A sense of betrayal

While most of us have many "emotional energy thieves," the most readily identifiable in second marriages are the old and new spouses, stepchildren and other relatives. Here are some common examples.

AN INWARD RESENTMENT

The husband resents his ex-wife for either her dependence on him or her efforts to control him. He resents her for their

The Dungeon

failed marriage, their ongoing court battles and perhaps the child support he pays. He resents his limited visitation and the fact he can't be with his kids more often. He may resent his new wife for insisting he break emotional ties with the ex-wife.

The new wife resents the ex-wife for trying to intrude in her new marriage and family. She resents her husband's inability to enforce boundaries with his ex-wife or his giving in to the stepkids. She also resents all the time and attention he gives the ex-wife. She may be annoyed by having to share their family income with the ex-wife and her children.

The ex-wife dislikes her ex-husband for having failed in the marriage, for refusing to cooperate with her demands or his late child support. Maybe she resents that he replaced her with someone younger, prettier or smarter. She is irritated with the new wife's influence over her children, or perhaps even resents the children when they begin to love their stepmom.

A Wounded Spirit

The husband feels hurt that his ex-wife refused to go to counseling or kicked him out. He is hurt that his children take their mother's side, or that they believe the bad things she says about him.

The new wife is hurt that her husband still seems to be attached to his ex-wife. She is hurt when the ex-wife refuses to be friendly or badmouths her to the children or other family members.

The ex-wife is hurt that her husband chose another woman over her. She is hurt when he doesn't seem to care about the children as much. Her spirit may be wounded when the children come home with stories about how pretty, funny, nice or smart their new stepmother is.

A Guilt

Both husband and ex-wife share burdens of guilt about their failed marriage, no matter who was more "at fault." A new wife may experience necessary and genuine guilt if she was involved with her husband prior to the divorce. All three parties, as they respond with other forms of bitterness, may feel various degrees of guilt for their past or ongoing actions.

AN ANXIETY/A FEAR

A husband who fears his ex-wife will take him to court for higher child support or reduced visitation is in bondage not only to her, but sometimes to the attorneys, mediators or judges.

An ex-wife who fears her husband will stop taking care of her or doing what he said he would do, is chained to him by bitterness. When she fears the children will love their step-mom more, she allows those children and their stepmom to become emotional energy thieves.

AN AVOIDANCE

A husband who makes his wife stay in the car when he drops the children off at his ex-wife's is avoiding uncomfortable situations. The new wife who doesn't want to go to "her" house to pick up the kids is in bondage to her as well. An ex-wife who won't speak to, look at or otherwise acknowledge her husband's new wife is allowing her to steal her serenity!

A SENSE OF ABANDONMENT/BETRAYAL

A husband whose ex-wife was unfaithful is usually still bitter. When the ex-wife takes him "to the cleaners" in court, he can feel betrayed by her, the attorney and the judge. When the kids want to live with their mother, the father may feel abandoned and betrayed.

The ex-wife can feel abandoned by her ex-husband in many ways. When he remarries, she feels betrayed. She can even extend this feeling to the new wife, who as woman-to-woman, never should have replaced her. When the children show love to their stepmother, these feelings resurface.

The Dungeon

The new wife most often feels abandoned when her husband takes the ex-wife's "side" in an issue, or when he spends time, money or attention that is rightfully hers on his ex-wife. Watching her husband share intimate memories with his ex-wife can stir up feelings of abandonment and betrayal. Hearing her new in-laws compare her with their "ex" daughter-in-law is also a source of such feelings.

WHAT'S THE SOLUTION?

Pull the plugs! Get rid of the "Rejection Connections" in your life. So far you've IDENTIFIED the root problems: the chains of bitterness, fear and guilt.

Now get ready to ISOLATE all the emotional energy thieves, be they people or circumstances. In the next chapter you begin to ELIMINATE the cords of bitterness which have kept you in bondage!

". . . where the Spirit of the Lord is, there is freedom."
2 Corinthians 3:17

Chapter 8

Breaking the Chains

❖

*"A person cannot break the patterns of the past until he is free
from the people of the past."* **Rejection Junkies**

While the main focus of this book is on the
new wife and the new marriage, it is important to reaffirm the effectiveness of these
principles for the former spouse. Smart strategies, careful
planning, attitude adjustments and prayer are useful tools for
anyone recovering from divorce.

The ex-wife may remarry and begin a blended family,
encountering similar joys and problems of her own. She may
also bear the brunt of an ex-husband's sporadic child support
payments or violation of the visitation agreement. But obviously not all problems in the new marriage can be blamed on
the former spouse. Though the marriage has been dissolved,
the problems that contributed to its failure do not magically
disappear. They may be lurking around corners of the new
relationship. Other people may have become a priority in a
new marriage, such as stepchildren or in-laws, best friends or
bosses. If any of these people are holding you or your spouse
as an emotional hostage, the patterns of your behavior need to
be altered and the chains of emotional bondage broken.

The Dungeon

The first action in the process of breaking the chains is to TAKE responsibility for our attitudes. Rarely are one's problems brought about solely by outside circumstances. Even when they are, circumstances cannot be controlled; our responses to them can. This chapter contains fifteen steps of acceptance, forgiveness and affirmation. For only when we seek and extend forgiveness can genuine healing and wholeness become reality.

STEP ONE

Accept the truth that God can, and wants to, meet all your emotional needs. God wants each of us to have a happy marriage and family life. More importantly, he wants us to lean on him.

STEP TWO

Accept the truth that you are human, have failed and will fail again. It's just a fact of life. The old habits of sin continue to affect us daily. But, like any other human failing, divorce should not keep us from continuing our fellowship with God, nor should it become a scarlet letter we wear for others.

STEP THREE

Accept the truth that other people, especially your ex-spouse and children, are also Rejection Junkies. They may continue to reject you. Nothing changes if nothing changes. You cannot control or be responsible for the behavior of others. You *can* control your own.

STEP FOUR

Accept the truth that you no longer need to react to other people's rejection. Instead, learn to respond by refusing to accept rejection or to believe others' attempts to shame you.

STEP FIVE

Accept the truth that what God thinks of you is important; what others think is not.

The second action in breaking the chains, is to SEEK for-giveness from others.

STEP SIX

Make a list of every single person, thing or circumstance of the past who has hurt, rejected, abandoned, betrayed or wounded your spirit. Guess what? You're not going to forgive them, for that is only part of the solution. You're going to ask forgiveness *from* them for your own bitterness toward them!

STEP SEVEN

Before you ask anyone to forgive you, pray this prayer out loud:
"Dear God, help me to turn _____'s response over to you so I don't come away feeling guilty or rejected."

First ask your NEW spouse to forgive you for 1) your bitterness and 2) for having failed as a husband/wife. Ask for a minute of private time. Hold his/her hand and keep steady eye contact. Use this script as a guideline:
"(Name), God has shown me that I need to ask your for-giveness for something. Will you forgive me for my bitter-ness toward you?"
"Will you also forgive me for having failed as your (hus-band/wife)?"

If you are not reading this book and working through the steps together, please follow the recommendations in Step Eight.

STEP EIGHT

Contact every person on your list and seek forgiveness for your bitterness. Begin with your ex-spouse.
This may be best done by using the telephone. *Always have your new spouse sit next to you for support and accountability.* There is a powerful bonding between husband and wife that occurs when they witness and encourage each other in true humility and emotional growth. Use this script as a guideline:

The Dungeon

"(Name), God has shown me that I need to ask you something. Will you please forgive me for my bitterness toward you?"

For ex-spouses, you need to also ask:

"Will you also forgive me for failing as a husband/wife to you?"

For your children, seek forgiveness in person, and try to sit on the floor or some lower level. This will capture their attention and keep them from being intimidated. Parents ask also for forgiveness for failing as a parent. Stepparents seek forgiveness for failing as a stepparent.

Never call or go alone when seeking forgiveness from an ex-spouse. This can be an emotional time, with past memories and feelings flooding the conversation. Deep eye contact can turn to hugs and kisses, which may be confusing and inappropriate. Old longings may resurface. Don't risk this. Having your new spouse by your side also speaks volumes about the end of the first relationship and the priorities of your head and heart.

Step Nine

Focus on your attitude, not their actions. Here are some suggested responses to possible reactions.

If They Say: What have I ever done to make you bitter?
You Say: It's not what you've done, it's that I've had the wrong attitude. Will you forgive me?

If They Say: What on earth are you talking about?
You Say: I need to ask forgiveness for my bitterness. Will you forgive me?

If They Say: Well, I don't know what you're trying to do.
You Say: I'm just asking you to please forgive me. Will you?

Only ask three times. If they keep trying to veer the conversation away from a direct answer to your question, then calmly use this closing statement:

"Before I called I turned over your response to God. I am not going to hang up feeling guilty or rejected. Good-bye."

This way you lay the "false guilt" at the other person's feet.

Don't discuss what they did. Remember, breaking the cycle of your old responses may confuse or scare the people you call. Don't focus on their actions or response, but on your own attitude.

Don't linger in the conversation. You're there to seek their forgiveness. If they can't or won't say, "Yes, I forgive you," God will not hold you responsible for their attitude or actions. End the conversation after three requests for forgiveness.

Don't try to counsel them. Once we experience the exhilarating freedom of true humility and forgiveness, we can be tempted to teach, lecture or explain to those we love or care about to get off the rejection cycle. Let God work in their lives through whatever means He chooses, in whatever timetable He intends.

Don't respond to their questions, comments or accusations. If an ex-spouse says, "I tried to be a good wife (husband), but you . . . ," just remain silent for a moment. If she hasn't forgiven you, use the closing statement and quietly hang up.

Don't get sucked into false "feelings" that your relationship with the other person will suddenly improve. In fact these calls may alienate some people from you. Remember, they are still caught in the Rejection Connection.

STEP TEN

Write letters to the people or things you cannot contact. Make a genuine effort to contact as many people of the past as you can. It is a very powerful and freeing experience to hear another human voice forgive you. It is also freeing to know the other person heard you seek their forgiveness, whether or not they give it. If this is not possible, write letters, even to inanimate objects or deceased persons.

STEP ELEVEN

Don't determine the success or failure of your actions by others' reactions. Whether they forgive you or not, mentally forgive yourself as God forgives you.

The Dungeon

STEP TWELVE

Thank God for your freedom from bitterness and make a commitment to never get in bondage to another person again! Delight in the knowledge that God loves and accepts you just as you are. Ask God to show you when you respond in bitterness in the future, and to help you avoid it.

The final action in the chain breaking process is to GRIEVE the loss of all that might have been.

STEP THIRTEEN

Bury the dead. I strongly recommend newly married couples hold a "memorial service" together to officially grieve marriages, dreams and hopes which have died. Flowers, lighted candles and prayers have soothed grieving survivors for centuries.

For husbands, gather the following:
Old photos of your ex-wife that you still might be keeping
Letters she has written you
Mementos of your old marriage
Clothing or other personal items she bought you that you still wear
Household items from your "old" life that you still have in your home
Anything and everything you possess that reminds you of your ex-wife

Now, make a list of all the dreams you held with your ex-wife, such as more children, the places you planned to travel, the hopes for a long marriage together. List the friends you lost and the other relationships that ended with your divorce. Transfer the list to a piece of paper. Sit down with your new wife and show her the items, explaining what they meant to you and how sad, hurt and disappointed you feel and why.

Ex-spouses may follow this procedure with their own list of broken dreams, quests for forgiveness and new goals. They may want to conduct their own private "funeral" for the failed marriage too.

New wives, do the same for your own hopes of getting along with his ex-spouse, his children, having to "share" your income with them, and any other hurts and disappointments resulting from your new marriage. Pray together asking God to heal your emotional wounds.

Schedule another "funeral" for the new wife's previous marriage which failed, if applicable. Keep the two services separate, allowing yourselves to focus more clearly on each.

Now take all the items, including the list of unfulfilled hopes and dreams and either bury them, burn them or take them to the dump. Don't leave them in the garage until the trash truck comes, like a body on ice. Give the "dead" a quick and proper burial. Donate valuable or useful items to your church or favorite charity.

Finally, when the chains are broken, LEAVE the past behind.

STEP FOURTEEN

Don't entertain old regrets or guilt feelings! When you find yourself thinking of the "old days," learn to quickly say to yourself, "I am dead to the past!" and let your thoughts turn to something in the present for which you are grateful.

As you begin anew, CLEAVE to your new spouse.

STEP FIFTEEN

Use affirmations which help reconnect you to your new spouse. If you start to have thoughts about the past marriage which pull you from the present, go tell your NEW spouse how much in love you still are with her. Go get or give a kiss or hug. *Words of love to someone in the present quickly blow away ghosts from the past.*

The Dungeon

A New Focus

Knowing the person who's rejecting us is really just hurt and scared like we all sometimes are, should allow compassion for them to come a little easier.

My husband and I got a new focus on our situation through completion of the "action therapy" of seeking forgiveness from each other and from his ex-wife. This poem may help you visualize the message of hope and peace this can bring:

God's Little Lecture

Sit down, you two, and listen well;
I have some things to say.
I know you wish she'd disappear,
So you could have your way.

She hasn't been too loving;
She's been unfair, it's true.
But through these trials I hope to build
Some character in you!

Get your focus off her
and start to look inside;
Start to change your attitudes
and get rid of that pride.

Learn not to fear rejection;
Learn new ways to reply.
Let go of your own bitterness —
The beam that's in your eye.

Quit trying hard to change her;
Don't try to take control.
Bear with the trials, keep the faith
and focus on your soul.

Just keep a grateful spirit.
Toward growth I'm pushing you.
All the things you think aren't fair
Are just my gifts to you.

Through suffering you'll find me;
Just keep a steady pace.
Look for the things that you can learn,
and I'll send you my grace.

You're my precious children,
But she's my daughter, too.
Just trust her to MY loving care;
I've plans for all of you.

When bitterness is gone, compassion and genuine caring can replace it. *Remember, though, having compassion for others does not mean receiving their rejection or tolerating their abusive behavior.* The next section of the book will help you keep the royal guard posted around your family castle so the arrows of future rejection can be deflected.

"Do not repay anyone evil for evil . . . If it is possible,
as far as it depends on you, live at peace with everyone."
Romans 12:17,18

Part II

The Castle Walls

"A Man's Home Is His Castle."

Sir Edward Coke - 1644

Chapter 9

Redefining Your Roles

❧✟❧

We can agree that physical distance is most appropriate after a man leaves home or gets a divorce. Why, then, do we have such a hard time agreeing that mental and emotional distance is also appropriate?

The Husband's New Role - Business Associate

You were her husband, but you're not now. If you have sought forgiveness for your failure and your bitterness, accepted yourself on the same level God does, and allowed yourself to grieve your losses, then you can move into your new marriage and close the door on the past relationship. *If you haven't completed these steps, the door will still be open.*

You can remain kind and courteous to your ex-wife, but you should keep communication and contact to a minimum and on a business level. This may sound pretty cold, but *it is the best approach* when there is continued hostility, manipulation or efforts at rekindling old roles. Spouses who continue sharing deep feelings and emotions, even negative ones, are still being "intimate" with each other.

The Castle Walls

Your contact with your ex-wife will usually include pay-ment of child support and other agreed expenses such as med-ical costs or life insurance. You'll exchange travel information when you take the kids on extended or out-of-state trips. You may exchange medical information because doctors may not release medical information to the noncustodial parent. How-ever, all these exchanges can be done through the mail like other bills. These items do not require hand delivery. Follow-up phone calls, if necessary, can and should be brief.

Business associates exchange information quickly to allow time for other assignments. In today's world, men rarely have enough time to devote to their job, wife, kids, home, yard, fam-ily budget, church or other groups. Therefore, to continue devoting energy to the ex-wife, with casual visits, extended phone calls or conversation is just not efficient use of a remar-ried man's time! His wife and new home should be first priori-ty, even above that 20-minute chat in his ex-wife's front yard while he tries to be "nice" and keep her "happy."

WHEN "BEING FRIENDS" IS NOT A GOOD THING

There's another reason why a husband should keep his relationship with the ex-wife to a minimum. Many ex-wives are still in emotional bondage to him. They secretly hope someday he'll "come to his senses" and leave the new wife, returning to them. What a husband perceives as being friendly and peacemaking, the ex-wife may interpret as caring on a more intimate level. A kind, but detached, method of commu-nication is sometimes the best thing a husband can do for his ex-wife.

Whether or not an ex-wife has any desire to get back with her ex-husband, all kids watch their divorced parents interact. Like little radar screens, they pick up voice tones, looks and body language while Mom and Dad talk. Even though they know Mom or Dad is remarried, and may even love their new stepparents, they still often dream of their "real" mom and dad getting back together. This is normal and only a reflection of that strong sense of family that God instills in all his children.

When Mom flirts with Dad, or Dad puts his arm around his ex-wife's shoulder, meant only as a casual nicety, painful emotions can be triggered in the children, and cause them to continue to carry false hopes. *The friendly, but businesslike relationship helps the kids accept reality faster.*

Husbands should also be sensitive to any insecurities their new wives have. If a new wife is struggling with feelings of inferiority as a new wife or stepmother, it can pain her to watch her husband share knowing looks or discuss old family times with his "ex." *When is that arm around the shoulder or casual peck on the cheek okay?* When the new wife is confident, when the ex-wife is emotionally healthy and reconciled to reality, and when the kids have accepted the fact that Mom and Dad will never get back together. Husbands should be aware this usually takes years to happen, if it ever does!

HUSBAND AND FATHER

A man's priorities after his relationship with God should be his wife and children, in that order. If a man has any extra time, attention, affection or energy, it should go first to his new wife.

Although his place of residence and his spouse have changed, a man's role as father never changes. He needs to continue doing the best job of parenting he can, even from afar, even on weekends. If a man honors his commitment to his children, God will send him the grace, strength and resources to parent his children the best way he can.

DEFINING A ROLE

Unlike unhealthy emotional distance, carved out of bitterness, a healthy avoidance stems from the realization that:
+ We can't go back to the past. Trying to recreate the happy feelings of the old relationship is only a temporary balm to unresolved past pain.

The Castle Walls

✦ Recreating familiar, friendly or emotionally intimate responses can lead the ex-spouse and the children to false hopes. When they remain in bondage to such hopes, they have no chance of emotional maturity.

The Ex-wife's New Role

"I hated it when my ex-husband wouldn't come in and visit for awhile," Sharon told me. "I'm not going to bite, for goodness sake! I just wanted to know how he was getting along and tell him about my folks' fiftieth wedding anniversary party. It's been so long since we've talked about anything on a friendly basis. Is that so bad?"

Sharon's comment is typical of divorced spouses who would like everything to seem "okay" again. After the fighting has calmed down, people seek the familiar. Many divorced women, like Sharon, feel that if they can resume some level of intimacy with their ex-husbands, he must still care or at least is no longer bitter. No one wants any more rejection.

However such feelings are artificial and incomplete unless the ex-husband reciprocates in that old friendly way. If he does not, the ex-wife remains in emotional bondage, seeking affirmation of her self-worth from her ex-husband.

With time, our memories of the unhappy times fade. We block the pain and tend to remember only the sweet times, often exaggerated in our minds. A man laughing and recalling better times with his ex-wife may suddenly feel the strong emotions they once shared. Thoughts of love, old embraces and nights of passion can ignite a spark in his mind. When he begins to entertain these thoughts, they can move to memories of bringing children into the world together and all the powerful bonds of marriage. Suddenly he's filled with doubt again. Do I still love her? Did I make a mistake? Feelings of failure and regret rise within him. This can cause him problems in his current marriage, or tempt him to renew levels of intimacy with his ex-wife.

The Daycare Lady

My husband shared a "word picture" of how he regards his ex-wife. When we don't know how to categorize our relationship with someone, it's helpful to say, "He's like a father to me," or "She's like a sister." My husband thinks of his ex-wife as the "Daycare Lady."

Imagine a nice lady who lives down the street. She owns the daycare center in your neighborhood. Every morning she drives to your house to pick up the kids. Sometimes you might drive to her house to drop them off. They get in her car and she takes them for the day. You relax and don't worry about them because you know she loves them and takes good care of them while they are with her. When they come home and report something fun or nice the "Mrs. Daycare" did for them, you appreciate it. You don't feel jealous. You know you are their parent and they will always love you, but they have room in their heart for her too. You are glad that your children have many adults in their lives to love, teach and care for them.

You and "Mrs. Daycare" sometimes smile and wave to each other in the mornings. Once in awhile she'll take a minute or two to report trouble with the kids' behavior and tell you how she's handling it during the day. You may stop and tell her about the children's rashes and leave the ointment with her for the day. You don't spend a lot of time talking to her when you pick the kids up, and you don't socialize on the weekends. You consider your relationship with her the same kind you'd have with a child's school teacher. While she is a trusted caregiver for the children, you have your own life, circle of friends and have no need to know more about or get involved in "Mrs. Daycare's" personal life. You don't tell her how to run the daycare center and she doesn't tell you how to run your home. *You have agreed to trust that you are each doing your job.*

Every month she sends you a bill and you mail her check out on time. That's the extent of your personal relationship with her.

The Castle Walls

This picture helps my husband honor his ex-wife for the role she has as mother to his son, and helps him encourage his son's loving relationship with her. It also helps him realize he doesn't need to be any more emotionally involved with her than he would be with "Mrs. Daycare."

The New Wife's Role

While she doesn't need to change an old role, the new wife assumes a very special role when she marries a man with children — stepmother. I call it the "other hand that rocks the cradle," due to the awesome potential for teaching and showing love in the new family, affecting generations to follow. But what happens when *two women* take turns loving, caring for and nurturing the same child?

I have been blessed to parent my stepson, Mike, every other weekend, once a week, half the summer and alternate holidays. Over the years I have:

loved him.

fed him.

bathed him.

taken him to the emergency room for stitches.

felt terror when I turned around in a store and he wasn't there.

helped him write his name, learn his numbers and ABCs.

taught him his first prayers.

held him in my arms when he cried.

held his two-wheel bike the first time he rode without training wheels.

spanked him with the authority of my husband when he was defiant.

hugged him afterward and told him I loved him.

taught him the Ten Commandments and his first Bible verse.

had slumber parties for him.

watched his baseball and soccer games.

helped him with his homework.

helped him pick out clothes.

cut his hair.

redecorated his room.
told him how much I love his father.
told him stories about when I was little.
kissed him good night and watched him sleep.
prayed for him.

I didn't have morning sickness, carry him for nine months or go through labor pains with Mike, but I am lucky to be a "real mother" to him in every other sense of the word.

Some stepmothers are not so lucky. They come into their stepchildren's lives when the children are older and these kids may have great difficulty bonding with or even accepting them as another "parent." Sometimes the children will blame the stepparent for the divorce, or for keeping Mom and Dad from getting back together. In many cases, an insecure or jealous ex-spouse will encourage the children to reject their stepparent. This can be painful and take a long time to work through, but does not diminish the fact that you are their stepmother.

Prayer, patience and sensitivity can help establish a relationship with the kids, but that's not all it takes. Just as with a successful marriage, it also takes lots of advice-seeking, soul-searching, counseling, reading, continuing education and practical application . . . and an understanding and sensitive husband!

The important thing to remember is that stepparents don't need their stepchildren's acceptance, approval or love to have a good marriage with their father. Stepparents do need, however, to continue to love and accept the stepchildren for who, what and where they are.

A New Wife's Hunting Expedition

Most men are notorious for not sharing their feelings and may have trouble communicating with their wives. Frequently newly married women will seek out their husband's mother for insights as to "what makes him tick." They believe that if they know some of their husband's history they may get to know him better.

The Castle Walls

Now who do you think would be the most likely person to report the inside scoop, the most up-to-date information on a divorced woman's husband? *His ex-wife, of course!* No one would know the intimate details better. Many new wives make the mistake of seeking out the ex-wife to obtain such information. Some ex-wives jump at the chance to share and thus remain up-to-date with what's going on in the new marriage.

This is trouble. The most common sharing is usually based on complaints. "Bill just comes home and plops down on the couch every night. Did he do that with *you?*" Soon the conversation turns to Bill's other weaknesses.

One of the most common things any woman does to undermine her marriage is to sit and run her husband down to her best friend, mother or sister. Women have a way of consoling and nurturing each other and satisfying each other's needs for conversation, communication and friendship. If a woman isn't getting these needs met primarily in her friendship, this confidante will become a "secondary spouse." Instead of going back to the husband and encouraging him to meet her conversational needs, it's easier for women to get it from each other. This detracts from the marriage bond.

Any woman who is jealous of a wife bonding with her new husband is exactly the woman in whom a wife should not confide. This includes mothers who were close to their daughters before the marriage, best friends who did everything together before she married him, and hurt, lonely, angry ex-wives.

THE BIG MYTH

Many people advise second wives to sit down and talk with his ex-wife before marrying him, or at the first sign of trouble. Ex-wives can supposedly give insight to the new wife. There are a few problems with this advice:

1) The new wife who is "in love" is not likely to be open to negative advice about the man she's ready to marry. People in love rarely listen to warnings about the pitfalls they may encounter in marriage.

2) Why should anyone take advice from a person they hardly know, or haven't learned to trust? Until you understand a person's own emotional background, you'll never know what their advice is based on, or how distorted their side of the story may be.

3) Since other women, even those who say they love our husbands (an ex-wife, girlfriend, mother or mother-in-law), are victims of rejection themselves, they may give the new wife advice colored by their own fears, hurts and anger.

Remember that ex-wives also carry guilt and shame about their failed marriage. Even though they may blame the ex-husband for the majority of the problems, they may not want him to succeed with a new wife. That would only send the message to the world that "he made it with *her*, but not with me." She may consciously or subconsciously try to undermine the new relationship whether she's "friends" with the new wife or not.

Remember too, *gossip is every woman's downfall.* What new wives tell the ex-wife (or anyone) in confidence may get back to the husband. The "Devil's Triangle" is not conducive to a successful new marriage.

The best advice a friend can give any wife, when she comes to unload her unhappiness with her husband is something to the effect of:

"I want to give you love and support, but I honor your marriage too much to sit and hear all these details. When I hear what you tell me about your husband, I get angry too. I don't want to get in a position to give you wrong advice. You're really the only one who knows what's best for your marriage. I'd like to encourage you to go back to your husband and tell him everything you were going to, or want to, tell me. I'll go shopping with you, watch the kids or come over and have coffee. But please don't tempt me to become your marriage counselor."

If you want information about your husband, plan some quiet time and ask *him.*

If you've got a complaint about him, approach him in a loving way and tell *him.*

If you want a satisfying friendship, make it with *him* first.

Chapter 10

Redefining Your Rights

◆

Joe wanted to send his son, Jeremy, who was in an average public school, to a nearby private school which had an excellent scholastic reputation. Some of his son's friends already attended the school, and it was close to the apartment where Jeremy lived with his mother, Joe's ex-wife. Joe was willing to pay full tuition on top of child support so there would be no financial burden on Jeremy's mother.

His ex-wife refused to even consider letting her husband have that much contact and influence over her son's activities. She'd been used to having full control, and only let Joe be involved as a parent every other weekend. In the past, when Joe had asked for extra time to take his son out for an ice cream after dinner, for instance, his ex-wife would refuse, saying, "It's not in the visitation agreement. You'll see him this weekend." She'd even told Joe to quit "harassing" her with requests for extra time with his son. "I only give you visitation because the court says I have to, Joe. All I really want is to be left alone with my son."

Joe's ex-wife complained about the driving inconvenience. "I agree it's a good school, but it's too far out of my route to work each morning," she argued. Joe offered, between him and his new wife, to provide transportation to and from school each day and have Jeremy home when she came home from work. But the ex-wife also didn't like Joe's new wife, and the last thing she wanted was for her son to be with Joe and his new wife every day to and from school.

"No," she continued, "After work I sometimes pick Jeremy up from daycare and we do things together in that part of town, like shop or visit friends. It's just too far out of my way to have to backtrack to that school every day."

"What about on days you have something planned if we agree to bring Jeremy to your office?" countered Joe.

"No, Joe, end of discussion!"

Joe's dilemma is a common one. After divorce, Joe lost the right to make decisions for and about his son. Unfortunately, with bitterness still in the way, the ex-wife did not choose what was best for her child's education, but what would protect her own emotional needs.

WHAT ARE YOUR LEGAL RIGHTS?

Parenting rights change with divorce. Your children either get to live with you or they don't. Many parents, usually fathers, retain the "right" to support their child financially, but lose their rights to see their children whenever they want.

Every divorced parent should have a good attorney who not only helps in the division of property, but who assists in structuring a working custody and visitation agreement. Most continuing problems between couples after their divorce, center around the custody and visitation arrangements.

This chapter is not intended as legal advice, but is a short summary of some of the considerations to be made in setting clear boundaries, regarding how you are to continue relating to an ex-spouse and parenting the children.

TYPES OF CUSTODY

Physical Custody is the right of a parent to have the child live with him or her. *Sole physical custody* is where the child lives with only one parent and "visits" the other. *Shared (or joint) physical custody* is where the child lives part time with Mom and part time with Dad.

Legal Custody is the right and obligation to make decisions regarding a child's health (mental, physical, spiritual), education and welfare. Although worded differently in different states, the intent is to make decisions such as where the child will go to school and what doctors they see.

Many parents share legal custody. Technically the noncustodial (or visiting) parent with "joint legal custody" gets to have equal input into where the child goes to school, for instance. In practice, though, if the two parents don't agree, it's the parent with sole physical custody who wins almost every time, like Joe's ex-wife. Unless the noncustodial parent has a compelling argument for the child's benefit, a powerful attorney, the court mediator's support and a sensible judge, he may be absolutely powerless over the outcome.

WHEN PARENTS CAN'T AGREE

If parents cannot agree on an issue, either parent can petition the court for help in making a decision. This is usually done by filing specific legal documents to bring the decision before the court. However, in an effort to reduce the number of petty arguments that would take up costly court time, many states require the parents to attend mediation. Some states, rather than require mediation, allow courts (the judge) to order mediation. In mediation, the court apppointed mediator will hear both sides and render a recommendation rather than a decision. Although the mediator has no legal authority to decide the outcome, judges who are too busy to educate themselves on family issues, or who have no way of telling who's telling the truth or not, will place nearly 100% reliance on the recommendation of the mediator.

Mediators are usually mental health professionals or attorneys trained in "conflict resolution." While there are some levelheaded, wise mediators in the system, there are also some

The Castle Walls

real "crackpots." They let each side talk and they try to calm emotions, but in the end may follow canned counseling formulas rather than common sense when making their recommendations to the couple or the court.

As parents, I urge you to try everything possible to come to some agreement rather than allowing total strangers, who themselves have their own prejudices, emotional problems and failed marriages, to make decisions about you and your children which will last a lifetime!

REASONABLE VISITATION

"Reasonable Visitation" is a catch-all phrase that gets written into divorce agreements by hasty lawyers or couples who think they will always be able to work things out fairly. Remember though, the marriage is ending usually because they weren't able to be fair or trust each other. Early divorce attitudes are often like honeymoon attitudes . . . they are based on hope and a promise things will go smoothly in the future. Like all honeymoon periods, this too will end.

Initially, many newly divorced couples who are tired of arguing and just want the other parent to know they want to "be friends" and "work together," will agree on this vaguely worded visitation agreement. They want to reassure each other they can be both trusting and trustworthy. The only problem is, since they couldn't trust each other, agree with each other or resolve conflicts in the marriage, they still won't outside the marriage. Why? Although their circumstances are now changed, their attitutudes, basic beliefs and values have not. Usually both of them are in emotional bondage and filled with one or more forms of bitterness.

"Reasonable Visitation" is a vague and open-ended agreement, ordering visitation for the child and their noncustodial parent at "reasonable times and places." This type of visitation agreement requires two mature, emotionally healthy adults who are free from bitterness to agree on where and when those places and times will be. The advantage of this open arrangement is that it provides flexibility in both parents' and children's schedules.

FIXED VISITATION SCHEDULE

A precise schedule is set up under this type of visitation order, and if the parents can't agree, the judge decides what days and times will be set. This is usually the type of solution ordered when parents display continued hositility toward each other.

The disadvantage is that visitation for the noncustodial parent can be severely restricted, and everyone's schedules will have to be reworked. The advantage, however, is if there is still an argumentative or uncooperative ex-spouse, there need be no argument if a court order sets specific days and times. The order must be followed or noncompliance will result in loss of visitation, fines, jail time, or even a change in custody. Chapter seventeen, "The Visitation Agreement," provides practical guidelines in building a workable agreement.

SUPERVISED VISITATION

Parents who have a history of drug, alcohol or other abuse, especially toward the child, may only be permitted to visit their child with another court-approved adult present. That adult may or may not be known to the parent or child, may be agreed upon by the parents, or may be ordered by the court.

GRANDPARENTS OR OTHERS' VISITATION

All states have laws which permit grandparents to seek visitation rights even if one or both of the parents disagree. Sometimes even former caregivers or stepparents will be granted continued visitation rights, depending on the extent of and nature of their relationship to the child.

VISITATION IS NOT JUST FOR MOM AND DAD

Some ex-spouses do not want their children visiting with former friends, neighbors or relatives of the other parent. One ex-wife tried to get visitation suspended when her children were with her husband for the weekend, but spent most of the

The Castle Walls

time with their stepmother because Dad was called away for the day and part of the evening on a medical emergency call. "Visitation is for the father, and nobody else!" she declared. The court disagreed. It is advantageous to spend time with stepparents, grandparents, aunts, uncles, cousins, friends, neighbors and other "extended family" members who have loving and healthy relationships with the children. While the court cautioned the father to make every effort to be with the children on his weekend, it was also understood that in real life that is not always possible. During visitation many children spend the night with Grandma, go to slumber parties, or stay with the babysitter, just as they do with the custodial parent.

STAY OUT OF COURT

While our founding fathers did everything they could to set up a fair legal system, it's far from perfect. Sometimes the courts will be there to protect you rights, while other times your rights will be violated, your requests vetoed. However, to make the most of the system in your state, I recommend the following:

Start Looking for a Lawyer

If you don't have one by now, get one! Call up a local counseling office and ask a staff counselor who works with family issues in court to recommend a few names. Ask other divorced couples you know whom they use and whom they recommend, as well as whom they don't recommend.

Your attorney should be as passionate about your rights as you are, and willing to aggressively pursue any and every means to help you. Make sure he explains exactly what he's doing and what you can expect from him and the courts. If you don't feel comfortable with him talk to him about your concerns. If he's still not meeting your needs, get someone else! Remember, your lawyer works for you!

Start a Library

Educate yourself so that you understand basic family law issues. Go to the bookstore/library and buy/check out all you can on divorce, custody and visitation issues. There are some good workbooks that show you how to modify or collect child support or change your visitation schedule. Search the Internet for home pages on divorce. Go to the message boards for church, family or legal support. Nolo Press has excellent publications both in the bookstores and on-line that cover many family law issues. Buy books and tapes that will help you sharpen your communication skills with the ex-spouse, the mediator and in court.

Start a Legal Fund

You can represent yourself in court and save thousands of dollars, but that is like performing your own brain surgery. For an action which could affect you, your spouse and your children for the rest of your lives, use a professional. Rework your family budget to set aside money each month for a legal fund. Talk to your attorney about costs of modifying support or visitation. Based on his/her advice, anticipate at least two to three times in court from the children's youth through the teen years. Start a savings account so when the time comes you're not hit with unexpected legal fees. Like the Boy Scouts say, "Be prepared!"

Start a List

Write everything down when the ex-spouse fails to show up on time, denies visitation or otherwise abuses the court orders. Log dates and time and reference notes. Keep records of abusive telephone calls and copies of messages on your recorder. Keep written letters you receive. Keep copies of all child support checks and other money paid to an ex-spouse. If you have to call the police, get a copy of the report. If you ever have to go to the court or the district attorney to change

The Castle Walls

custody, modify visitation or file a complaint, it helps to have documentation.

RIGHTS & RESPONSIBILITIES

In today's society people constantly demand their rights, but hardly a word is mentioned about responsibilities. Rights and responsibilities are like coins, two-sided and inseparable. One always comes with the other. If divorced and remarried people want a legal or any other type of right, they should also be prepared to shoulder the collateral responsibilities. The next chapter helps define those responsibilities.

Chapter 11
Redefining Your Responsibilities: What Not to Do

"**Y**ou are NOT picking up your son until after the party!" Bill's ex-wife screamed into the phone. With that she slammed down the receiver.

Bill took a deep breath and sat there for a minute. "Okay," he thought to himself, "Now what?"

Bill lived a few blocks away from his ex-wife and ten-year-old son, Jesse. As a result, Bill and his new wife were able to be involved in many of Jesse's school, sports and other activities.

Bill's son, Jesse, had been doing poorly in school. He was a bright kid, but had been ignoring his teacher in class and was spending far too much time talking and joking with his classmates. His grades were falling. The teacher had sent several notes home and had put Jesse in detention. Although he'd missed recess a few times as a result, Jesse continued his disruptive behavior.

Bill was concerned. The last two years Jesse's teachers had gone through the same problems, and had sent the same message home: Jesse disregards the classroom rules. Bill realized Jesse's disobedient behavior had become habitual. He knew how important it was to help break Jesse's habit before he reached adolescence and the teen years. Such behavior, if left unchecked, could grow into willful defiance and eventually, rebellion.

Trying to decide the best motivation for changing his son's attitude, Bill thought about baseball. Jesse loved baseball and was one of the star players on his little league team. His mother had always encouraged his sports and was proud to have her son on the best team in the league this year. So far this season they were in first place.

"I'm going to call your teacher twice a week," Bill told his son. "If she reports poor behavior on your part, you will not be able to play the next baseball game. If you start to follow directions and pay attention, there will be no problem. Got it?"

"Yeah, Dad." Jesse said.

"You are in control here, son. If you miss a baseball game, it will be because of your own choices. It's time to start taking responsibility for your attitude and your actions."

Bill's ex-wife was furious that he was threatening to use the baseball games to discipline Jesse. Despite Jesse's young age, his mother had already made it known she intended Jesse to go to college on a sports scholarship.

"He has a commitment to his team, Bill. You can't take his games away. The coach and everyone else are depending on him to win the games. Why don't you just spank him instead?" she asked.

"Because spanking obviously hasn't worked in the past on this. Discipline isn't effective unless kids lose something that's really important to them. With Jesse, it's baseball."

His ex-wife's voice tightened. "I'll never forgive you for this. You don't care about his sports. You're only hurting him and the team! You're not taking away any games that fall on my weekends!'

"If he behaves in school, he won't miss *any* games," Bill reminded his ex-wife. "Jesse needs to learn that school is the most important thing in his life right now, not baseball. He needs to learn responsibility for his behavior."

Jesse did fine for a few weeks, then his teacher reported

problems in the classroom. There was only one game left that season and the pizza party afterward. They fell on a Friday night of Bill's weekend visitation with his son.

Bill's visitation officially started after school on Fridays. The last game started at 6:00 p.m. and the party followed. Bill decided that Jesse could attend the game but would miss out on the party as the consequence for his disobedience at school. Jesse was crushed, but accepted his Dad's decision.

Bill's ex-wife, however, thought she could prevent Bill from taking his son home before the party. Since they would be in public, she figured Bill would give in to her. As soon as the game ended, she ran over and told Jesse to get in her car and she'd take him to the party.

"But what about Dad, Mom?"

"Just forget about it. I'll take care of him. Get in the car."

Jesse's mother whisked him away to the local pizza parlor where the team was meeting for their party. Not wanting to put Jesse in a physical tug-of-war, Bill calmly went to the pay phone, called the sheriff and waited until he arrived. Bill showed him the copy of the court visitation agreement he kept in his car, and the sheriff escorted him to the pizza parlor. The sheriff asked Bill to remain in the car. In a few minutes he returned with Jesse, who was carrying his backpack and base-ball gear.

"Hi, Dad," Jesse said slowly, but understandingly.

"Hi, Son. Hop in."

WHY WE NEED BOUNDARIES

Did you see the movie Jurassic Park? On a mist-shrouded island in the Pacific Ocean, scientists were secretly breeding all kinds of dinosaurs, including a ferocious Tyrannosaurus Rex. The only thing between the scientists' headquarters and the hungry dinosaurs was a tall cyclone mesh fence. Not very formidable in structure, the fence nevertheless was very effective in keeping the dinosaurs on the other side. Why? Because there was a powerful electric current running through the fence, and anytime a dinosaur touched the fence, he was zapped!

About half-way through the movie, the worst happened: the electricity went out and T-Rex effortlessly knocked down the fence and started gobbling up the scientists!

This movie scene illustrates the most important principle about boundaries. *It's not the boundary that keeps the intruder out, it's the consequence of overstepping the boundary that keeps him away.* The wire fence was flimsy. The fence only represented the line that was drawn between the two sides. The real boundary was the electric charge that caused the dinosaurs pain.

Telling an ex-wife that she should have the children at your home at 7:00 p.m. is just "the line" you draw. If the ex-wife knows she will not suffer in any way if she arrives an hour late or not at all, your "boundary" is no better than that invisible line. If, however, she knows there is an electric current (you will call the sheriff, file a complaint with the District Attorney, or that she may be fined or put in jail) she's more likely to respect the boundary.

ESCALATING THE ATTACK

Some animals will still charge the fence. We hear stories of pit bulls and rottweilers that go crazy with rage and attack barbed wire or electric fences despite the pain. These animals are "crazy" and usually end up killing themselves. That's not brave; that's stupid. Unfortunately, we humans can be just as stupid.

It's not uncommon for anyone setting a new boundary to experience greater attack. Ever notice when you say no to the kids, they keep asking, then start to beg or plead? After that they may try another tactic, like tantrums or anger. Be prepared for an increase in the intensity of "attack" when you try to stop an angry ex-spouse. Hold firm. Be ready to go the distance, or they will wear you down to the point you give in. When that happens, you lose your self-respect and that of those around you.

Redefining Your Responsibilities: What Not to Do

DON'T LET GUILT KEEP YOU FROM SETTING BOUNDARIES

A "good" ex-husband, a "good" father are what many men really want to be after a divorce. Unfortunately, Webster doesn't clearly define these terms, and society has muddled their meaning. Many men will go overboard in their assumed obligations and duties to the ex-wife and children. Why? Some by their nature are caretakers and derive self-esteem from this role. Others perform out of guilt, whether genuine or false. Remember their definitions in chapter four?

False Guilt *is anxiety created by a fear of rejection from a lack of performance.*

Genuine Guilt *is a grieving created by the Holy Spirit over a situation.*

You don't have to buy your kids everything the ex-wife tells you to buy because she can't afford it and you can. Kids shouldn't always have everything they want, or what an angry mother thinks you should buy them. Instead, pray for discernment to decide what is appropriate and what is not. Your wife will probably have some wise counsel in this area. These can be good opportunities to teach your kids *delayed gratification,* working for what they want or learning how to accept "no" for an answer, skills they will need all their lives!

You don't have to stop what you're doing when they call; if it's not an emergency and you need to finish something of importance, it's OKAY to tell them you'll call back later. Just make sure you honor all your commitments.

WHEN NEW WIVES ARE STILL IN BONDAGE

Like any woman, you want a happy home with lots of love for all. You want your husband to love you and think you're wonderful. You want your stepchildren to love you, and you want a cordial relationship with the ex-wife. It might happen in Hollywood, but in real life it happens only rarely. Many people claim they "get along fine," but it's often because there hasn't been a crisis recently, or they're afraid to acknowledge

The Castle Walls

their true feelings for fear of rejection. It takes all three adults having reached a level of maturity most people never achieve. We need to learn to let go of those fariy-tale images and accept that some people might not love you, might reject you, might even hate you, and that's okay. Another person's feelings about us are just that — their own feelings.

We don't have to like someone to love them. It's okay not to want to be around someone who resents or hates you. In fact, it's wise to stay clear of people who have threatened you physically or who abuse you verbally. The problem is not yours; it's theirs. They are responsible for their feelings or actions, and you were not put on earth to control others' feelings. You are here, though, to respond in love, tempered with safe boundaries. Your only responsibility is to be kind, honest, open and free from bitterness. You can get angry, yes, but vent and let it go. Keep your focus not on her actions but on your own attitude. *You may not be able to forget, but you should always forgive her.*

THE HUSBAND'S RESPONSIBILITIES

After divorce, the husband's responsibility to the ex-wife should be limited only to fulfilling the obligations set upon him by the courts, namely payment of child support and/or alimony, and adhering to the visitation agreement. These obligations *are to the children*, not to the ex-wife. There's a difference. Although the role as *father* should always continue, the *husband* role has ended.

WHAT HUSBANDS AND NEW WIVES DON'T HAVE TO DO FOR THE EX-WIFE

"Dad, how come you won't help Mom?" asked Brett's nine-year-old son, Matt.

"What do you mean, Matt?" asked Brett. Matt told his dad how he had overheard his mother on the phone with her sister, bitterly complaining about her ex-husband's refusal to help her put up the Christmas lights. Brett's ex-wife, Sue, had not remarried and was not the type to scale an eight-foot ladder and hang lights around the housetop.

"Mom said she can't hang the lights and *you* won't help her. She said you did last year and now you're just being mean. And she called you a bad name, Dad." Brett smiled and tousled Matt's hair. "It's okay, Son. I'm sorry your mom's angry, but I can't help how she feels. Your mom can hire someone to help her put the lights up. I sent her a little extra money this month just for that."

"Yeah, but Mom said she's not gonna hire someone when you can do it. She said your new wife gets her lights put up but not us. She said if you don't do it, we won't have lights this year. Dad, all us kids really want the lights up!"

Brett sat his son down and looked him square in the eye. "Son, I am not responsible for your mother or her house anymore. I am responsible for you kids and I will always make sure I take care of you the best I can. Your mom needs to stop having you kids ask me to do things that she can take care of herself or get someone else to do, like Uncle Bob or her dad. *She's responsible for what you guys want, too.* My first responsibility is taking care of your stepmom, Ginny, and keeping our house up. When you guys come to visit, we'll have lights here. Understand?"

"Yeah." Then Matt got teary-eyed. "Dad . . . you don't love Mom anymore, do you?" Brett put his arm around Matt. "Son, I care very much about your mom and always will. But I need to let her be responsible for her own life now. She's a very bright and capable person, and I'm no longer responsible for her. I'm sorry this hurts. I know you're still sad about the divorce. But I love you more than I ever did, and I'll always be here if you need me." He waited a moment. "Do you need to tell me anything else, Matt?"

Matt snuggled into his dad's chest and was quiet for a moment. "No, Dad. I love you too."

There are probably many things you may have done or are still doing for the ex-wife that you no longer have to, or should, keep doing. See how many of these you can identify in your own situation:

The Castle Walls

Don't force yourself or pretend to like her or be friends with her.

You don't have to try to keep her happy.

Don't hand deliver the child support each month.

You don't have to pick up groceries for her on your way over.

You don't have to pick up or take the kids somewhere if she is physically able.

Don't fix her car.

Don't lend her money.

Don't pay her bills.

Don't put up the Christmas tree, fix the roof or move the piano.

Don't keep her on your credit cards.

Don't keep her name on the business.

You don't have to help her move to a new apartment or house.

You don't have to hug or kiss her.

You don't have to try to make interesting conversation with her.

Don't "act" friendly and happy toward her if you don't feel like it.

You don't have to take her to the airport.

Don't pay *all* the extra medical or dental bills.

Don't pay for all the extras the kids want.

You don't need to stay in touch with her family.

You don't need to stay in touch with her friends.

You don't need to attend school functions or conferences together.

You don't have to sit by her at functions where the kids are involved.

You don't always have to send the kids' clothes home washed and folded.

You don't have to have the kids wear what she sends over.

You don't have to explain all your actions to her.

You don't have to trade or change visitation times to meet her schedule.

You don't need to take abuse or harassment just because you're the noncustodial parent.

Don't let your new wife handle your responsibilities.

Don't rely on her to get school or sports information to you.

This is a way an angry ex-wife can control the situation. If you want to keep in touch with the school, make direct and separate contact. If you want to talk to the baseball coach and get a game schedule, do it. Don't wait for the ex-wife to do so. Some ex-wives really wish their ex-husband weren't involved with the kids at all and will make sure Dad doesn't get notification of anything. When fathers ask for information, withholding provides her with a way to overcome her feelings of powerlessness, especially if she still feels victimized by her ex-husband.

Give the teacher self-addressed stamped envelopes to send you weekly progress reports or notices about school pictures. When she signs the children up for sports, give the coach your name, address and phone numbers.

If you need a copy of their birth certificate, contact the county registrar yourself. If you need a copy of the children's social security numbers, contact the agency directly. If you need copies of medical or dental records, ask the court to help you get copies from the doctors. (Most doctors will not release information to the other parent, even with joint legal custody).

You don't need to let the kids talk to her every single time she calls.

Be discerning. Younger children may need to talk to their mothers more frequently, but overly attached children who need to start bonding with Dad may need to wean themselves from Mommy's frequent calls. Children need to go longer stretches at a time away from Mom or Dad as they get older.

Listen to their phone calls. Does the child turn whiny or cry afterward? Does his or her mood change after talking to Mom? Consider the child's responses when making your decisions about permitting the phone calls. Even if the court order directs you to provide "open telephone access," *you* are the parent and often a better judge of the phone call situation than the court. Keep it reasonable, and keep it fair.

If you're not sure how to respond to a request from your ex-wife, ask yourself these questions:

✦ Can she do it herself without physically harming herself or the children?

The Castle Walls

+ Can someone else easily do it for her (family, friend, neighbor)?
+ Will doing it make your new spouse uncomfortable?
+ Will doing it mislead or confuse your children and/or your ex-spouse?
+ Will doing it take away time, attention or money that should first go to your new spouse?

JUST FOR STEPMOTHERS

Don't assume moral responsibility for the kids' upbringing.

The children's father and mother are responsible for their upbringing. Your role is to love the children, set and enforce healthy boundaries for them, yourself and your family, and to accept the children as they are. You can advise your husband when you have some insight to their behavior or problems. You can teach them and encourage their growth as you would your own children.

You are responsible, though, for giving wise counsel from your experience, and insight and support to your husband regarding the children. How he responds to your counsel and the children's needs is his responsibility, and you may need to sit back and allow him room to make mistakes.

Don't sit back and let your husband flounder.

One of the first reactions a stepmother who's just been rejected by the stepchildren will have is withdrawal. When they reject you, or don't respond to your nurturing or guidance, go have a good cry on your husband's shoulder, get away from the kids for awhile, but don't give up on them. They *really* want you to hang in there with them, they just don't know it yet!

Don't take a back seat as stepparent.

Even if the kids reject you, or their mother tries to turn them against you, continue to enforce your household boundaries and continue to love them as they are. You can and should discipline your stepchildren through your husband's authority when appropriate. This, too, is a way of loving the kids! The children need to see you and your husband are an inseparable team and are both committed to providing firm discipline and lots of love. This will help give them the security all kids crave.

Don't force the kids to call you "Mom" or any form of "Mom."

The kids have one biological mother. If you can't honor her, at least honor her rightful position as their mother. Kids get too confused with "Mommy Carol" and "Mommy Ann," or "Dad and Daddy." Stepparents should be secure enough not to make the children call them "Mom" or "Dad." Using these titles may be perfectly appropriate if the ex-wife is dead, or doesn't have custody and lives far away and the kids have rarely seen her. Sometimes the kids feel comfortable calling a stepparent Mom or Dad because all the other kids do. However, stepmoms can act like a mother, love like a mother, and receive the kind of love a child gives a mother, WITHOUT the title.

Don't hog the front seat as a stepparent.

It is very easy for any married man to let his wife handle raising the children. Even if you, the stepmother, have a knack for parenting and are in tune with the children, allow their father to be involved as much as you are with the children. Husbands, don't let your new wife have the "lion's share" of babysitting, teaching or nurturing your children just because she's good at it or it's easier. Those kids need YOU.

Don't assume your husband's responsibility.

Don't remind him the child support is due. Let him be late and learn the consequences of his own behavior. Don't remind him to go pick up the kids on time. Let him schedule that into his own timetable, and if he's late, let him suffer the consequences. If the consequences include an angry ex-wife, admonishment by the court, or worse, fines, jail, or loss of visitation, that's HIS problem to deal with. Otherwise your husband will either start to depend on you or will resent what he hears as "nagging." Don't become either his mother or his conscience. Neither are healthy. *Would you like him reminding you to get the groceries, cook dinner and pick the kids up from school?*

Don't write out the child support check.

Although many wives handle the money and pay the bills, let your husband write out the support check. There is a psychological benefit to him to be reminded each month that he IS taking care of his children in this area and need not feel "guilty." It is emotionally satisfying for the ex-wife to see the signature on the check in *his* handwriting (not yours). Many ex-wives would rather not see the new wife taking care of an especially sensitive area that she might feel is her ex-husband's responsibility. She may feel that if he never sees that check go out, he doesn't really care about his financial responsibility. This may not be the case, but it's a courtesy to the ex-wife and an emotional benefit to the husband.

Don't try too hard.

Give the stepmother role all the love and energy you have, but don't get on a performance trip for your husband, the kids or their mother. No matter how hard you try, sometimes the children will not respond to you. This will only set you up to become bitter. Learn to go with the flow!

Don't defend yourself to the ex-wife.

Some ex-wives leave nasty messages on the phone recorder about the new wife. Some write letters to the ex-husband trying to drive a wedge between them. Some falsely accuse stepmothers to the extended family or friends. This is a time for the husband to stand up for or verbally defend his new wife, when necessary and in an appropriate manner. Let the responsibility of defending the wife fall back onto the husband's shoulders!

Redefining Your Responsibilities: What Not to Do

A WORD ABOUT CONFLICT

Husbands and wives should learn the difference between "disagreements" and "conflicts":

Disagreements center around attitudes.

Opinions, perceptions of reality or blaming are disagreements that don't have to be solved. Some ex-wives think their husbands are irresponsible, some husbands think their ex-wives are too permissive with the children. Conflicts may arise as a result of these attitudes, but the attitudes themselves don't necessarily require resolution.

Conflicts center around actions.

Once a person threatens to or acts in a manner that deprives the other of his or her needs or wants, whether real or perceived, then conflict occurs. Sometimes conflict can't be satisfactorily resolved, but it can be managed by our response.

BEFORE RESPONDING TO CONFLICT

Chapter 14, "Being Willing to Lose in Order to Win," provides instruction in specific problem solving. However, in negotiating day-to-day schedule changes, managing conflict, considering requests or other common communications with an ex-wife, always follow these steps:

1) Look at *all* the options, as unusual or unfamiliar as they may seem. Have you gathered all the facts first? Is there something new you can try? What will be the results?

2) What are your family priorities? Do you have a family "mission statement" or "constitution?" Make a list of family priorities if you don't have one. Which of the options you are considering in each situation fits best with family goals?

3) Always seek your spouse's input or suggestions.

4) Take time to decide how you will respond to a request or proposed schedule change. If you don't have to come up with an answer right away, don't. Allow yourself time to rethink the situation instead of reacting in old patterns.

Chapter 12

Redefining Your Responsibilities: What to Do

✦

hile knowing what not to do will protect you from many missteps, it is equally important to have an understanding of the positive actions you can take to smooth the path ahead as you forge new relationships among all parties concerned.

HUSBAND, SEEK YOUR EX-WIFE'S FORGIVENESS FOR FAILING AS A HUSBAND.

As we discussed in Part I, seek forgiveness for any wrong doing on your part in the marriage. Then, move on. If you haven't yet done your "action therapy," do it!

NEW WIFE, SEEK HER FORGIVENESS FOR ANY BITTERNESS YOU'VE HAD TOWARD HER.

Were you involved in an affair with him before their marriage ended? While this is something for which you need to take responsibility and seek forgiveness, adultery doesn't necessarily mean the marriage had to end. You may have played a part, but you are not solely responsible for the failure of *their*

The Castle Walls

marriage. No "other woman" is so powerful that she can ruin a marriage, and no man is so weak that he cannot resist her. People aren't forced to end their marriages; they make choices. *People do what they want to, nothing more, nothing less.* Claim responsibility and seek forgiveness for your own actions, not those of your husband.

DO WHATEVER THE COURTS TELL YOU TO DO.

If you don't like the results of court orders, either get an attorney who can help, or complete the grieving process *(anger, guilt and grief give way to acceptance, release and recovery)* by accepting the situation.

PAY CHILD SUPPORT IN FULL AND ON TIME.

Too many husbands are tempted to use this to get even with their ex-wives for something they withheld from them. Don't even *think* about it! This money's for the kids. You can't control how she spends it. Let go.

TREAT HER WITH COMMON COURTESY.

Try to remember this even when she's at her nastiest. You obviously could not get along well when you were married, and until you're both able to keep from falling back into old emotional habits, keep an emotional "arm's length." If she's being particularly unpleasant, recite, *"I DON'T* have to react to this!" or "I am dead to this!"

GIVE HER AS MUCH ADVANCE NOTICE OF PLANS AS YOU CAN.

Even though she may never warn you of last minute changes in plans, even though she may never give you information until the last minute, don't do the same to her! This is a good way you can "love" an ex-wife on a healthy level. Treat her with common courtesy.

Redefining Your Responsibilities: What to Do

NEVER LIE TO HER.

Even though she may lie to you, never mislead or confuse her deliberately.

Never fight in front of the kids.

Keep a cool head. When you feel the temperature rising, take a walk, go home, or take a break. Remind yourself, "I have options," "I can deal with this later," "I can give myself time to respond," or whatever works for you.

DON'T ACT SNOTTY OR GIVE HER THE COLD SHOULDER.

This is a normal response when we are bitter toward someone. Have you become bitter again? You might have to do action therapy a few times, especially with the ex-wife. If, however, you find yourself becoming bitter repeatedly, you really need to look at your own attitude. Remember: *anger is a response*, a normal and natural emotion in unfair situations. Process it, find a solution, if any, and let it go. *Bitterness is resentment*, a habitual attitude.

NEVER ALIENATE THE CHILDREN FROM HER.

It's natural for both divorced parents to try to get the kids on their "side." Let the kids love her and never alienate their affection for her. Do be honest, though, about your anger or frustration with her. Don't pretend you're happy as a clam if you're not. Kids see right through that. Kids *know* how you feel before you tell them! Children have a natural intuition for what's right or fair. In their hearts they will know. Give them time.

SET HEALTHY BOUNDARIES AND RISK HER DISFAVOR IF YOU HAVE TO ENFORCE THEM.

Do what you think is right and stick with it. Don't fear her anger, retaliation or revenge.

The Castle Walls

DO HELP OUT WHEN YOU CAN IF THERE IS AN EMERGENCY WITH THE KIDS.

Although it's healthy to cut emotional and other ties with the ex-wife, don't go to an extreme. Any time humans change their behavior, there's a tendency to let the pendulum swing too far to the other side. If there is a real emergency which affects the kids, by all means lend your time, energy and support!

TEACH THE KIDS YOUR PERSONAL BELIEFS; INSTILL VIRTUES IN THEM.

All parents are called to do this for their children or stepchildren. Even if you feel overwhelmed by their mother's lack of moral guidance for the kids, do what you can when they're with you. Every little bit will help. Pray that God will put others in their lives to take up the slack. It's okay to refute her values to them, just don't personalize it. Make it clear you reject *her values*, or lack of them, but that you don't reject *her*.

GIVE THE KIDS BOUNDARIES AND BE WILLING TO RISK THEIR ANGER AS A RESULT.

"Mom never makes us do that!" is frequently heard in blended families. Just smile and say, "I know that's how she does it, but we do it differently." Period.

If she's late bringing the children home, or refuses to let you pick them up, call the appropriate law enforcement agency. While most of these get tired of domestic calls, they are used to helping parents enforce their visitation order.

DO WHATEVER YOU HAVE TO DO TO KEEP YOUR MARRIAGE STRONG.

As I've said before, this is THE BEST gift you can give your children.

BE FAIR.

Don't get even. Don't be selfish. Being "fair," though, allows you to have the advantage sometimes without guilt. After all, you may have lost the privilege of having your children live with you. In all fairness, there are advantages you should enjoy without guilt. In "splitting" Christmas vacation, for example, don't feel guilty that you get more days than she does, or that you have the prime time. Fairness goes BOTH ways.

IF YOU'RE THE ONE WITH PHYSICAL CUSTODY, BE GENEROUS WITH EXTRA VISITATION.

Remember the biblical principle — do unto others as you would have them do unto you? Obey it.

DON'T COMPETE FOR THE KIDS' LOVE.

They have enough for all their parents — and more beside!

PRAY FOR THE KIDS; PRAY FOR HER.

Pray for them and with them. Let them hear you pray for their mother. Thank God in front of them for all the good she does for them. Mean it.

FORGIVE THE EX-WIFE IF SHE EVER ASKS.

She may never ask, and that's okay. If she does, extend her honest forgiveness as God does for you.

LET THE CHILDREN AND THEIR MOTHER HAVE PRIVACY.

Don't interrogate the kids about their mom or other home life. Don't ask them to keep secrets from her about you or what goes on in your family. Encourage them to talk about

The Castle Walls

anything they want with her. Don't do it, though, to get them to talk to you about her.

ASSUME WHAT THE KIDS TELL YOU IS NOT ALWAYS TRUE, OR MAY BE EXAGGERATED.

"Mom said . . ." If they report something their mother said or did that concerns you, check with her before jumping to conclusions.

EXPECT THE KIDS TO TELL YOU WHAT YOU WANT TO HEAR.

As they get older, kids will know exactly what you want to hear, and to avoid your rejection, will tell you what pleases you. They will tell you how mean their mom is to them, then turn around and tell her the same thing about you! It's their way of surviving in both households, and avoiding rejection by the people they love the most: all their parents!

ENCOURAGE THE CHILDREN IN THEIR LOVE AND RESPECT FOR THEIR MOTHER.

When they're little, help them buy her mother's day cards, birthday or Christmas presents. If she's remarried, though, let the new husband help them.

GIVE HER ADDRESSES/PHONE NUMBERS IN CASE OF EMERGENCY, ESPECIALLY WHEN YOU TRAVEL.

The ex-wife doesn't need to be calling you on your vacation. If the kids really miss her, let them call occasionally, definitely not every day. If she has the habit of calling frequently, give her the number of the front desk of the hotel, or other number where you can retrieve messages rather than be interrupted.

Redefining Your Responsibilities: What to Do

BRING THE KIDS HOME AND PICK THEM UP ON TIME.

Honor your legal and personal commitments. Show the kids what commitment means. If you can't avoid being late, stop to call her. Don't blame the traffic. Take responsibility (especially in front of the kids)! if your late arrival was something you could have avoided. Apologize.

STEPMOM, STAY OUT OF ANY ARGUMENTS BETWEEN YOUR HUS-BAND AND HIS EX-WIFE.

Although he may need your insight or counsel, talk to him before or after actual or potential confrontations; don't assume his responsibility in dealing with her.

STEPMOM, STAY HOME DURING LEGAL PROCEEDINGS.

Help your husband get ready for court; type, file or role play what he'll say. Offer your counsel. Help him find a good attorney. Pray for him and send him off with a kiss, but stay home and let him do his battle with her alone.

NEW WIFE, ENCOURAGE YOUR HUSBAND TOWARD RECONCILIATION WITH HER.

While it may not be possible now, or even in the near future, a man's wife should nevertheless be smart enough to know some type of eventual reconciliation would be best for him and the children. If *he's* smart enough, he'll recognize your maturity and love you even more!

NEVER GIVE UP ON TRYING TO RECONCILE WITH YOUR FORMER SPOUSE

We are called to be reconciled one to another. It's not a request; it's vital to our spiritual and emotional health. However, reconciliation takes TWO and it takes TIME. Reconciliation will

The Castle Walls

not occur until and unless both parties have an "open spirit." If your former spouse is not receptive to reconciliation on any level, give him/her a few weeks, months or even years.

If we can't be reconciled to the *relationship*, we can be reconciled to reality. The *reality* is that it may take time, or it may never happen. To continually push her into reconciliation may be no more than a form of control and even harassment!

Chapter 13

What You Can and Can't Control

❧✦❧

Jim's fourteen-year-old daughter, Tina, had wanted her ears pierced since she was ten. Tina's mother, Mary, was adamantly against the ear piercing, for reasons that were never quite clear. Jim suspected it was because his new wife, Barb, had taken Tina under her wing the last five years and had developed a loving stepparent relationship with Tina. Barb was the first one to suggest Tina get her ears pierced and offered to buy her first pair of gold earrings!

After two years of begging and pleading with her dad, Tina was delighted when he agreed to let her have her ears pierced the next day. Jim called his ex-wife and advised her he thought it was time to honor Tina's request. Mary flew into a rage. "Don't you dare pierce my daughter's ears or I'll have you in court faster than you can blink!" She slammed the phone down and refused to pick up when Jim called her back.

Jim had honored Mary's request for several years, but now made the decision to exercise his legal rights. Piercing Tina's ears would bring her pleasure, was not illegal, immoral or indecent, and he could see no potential problem, except for Mary. Although he wanted to respect Mary's feelings as the

The Castle Walls

other parent, Jim considered himself an equal parent, despite his limited time with Tina. He knew there would be trouble, and that Tina would suffer as well when she went home to her mother.

Jim was emotionally free from Mary, though, and was not afraid to "cause" a problem with his ex-wife. He wasn't about to be controlled by her rage. Jim gave Barb fifty dollars and told her to take Tina to get her ears pierced and out to lunch. Barb and Tina giggled excitedly as they drove off to the mall. Tina came home that afternoon, feeling very grown up and very pretty. "Thanks, Dad," she said, grinning.

That night, before taking Tina to her mom's, Jim told Tina to be prepared for her mother's anger. "I'm sorry you have to go through this, honey, but we all need to learn not to stay in fear of people who get angry at us. Your mother's anger is at me, and I will deal with it the way God wants me to. I hope you will not react to your mom's anger, or feel guilty. Remember how we talked about genuine and false guilt? Let your mom have her reactions, but you remember to take a deep breath and know you're okay and that we ALL love you! Call me if you need to talk, okay?"

Two days later a registered letter came from Mary to Jim and Barb. Mary's anger was usually directed at the new wife, whom she blamed for all the trouble between her and her ex-husband. Mary had convinced herself that Jim would not keep rejecting her if Barb was out of the picture. Desperately wanting her ex-husband to still "like" her, she vented her anger at Barb. In her letter Mary accused Barb of trying to turn Tina against her and blasted Jim for letting his "controlling wife" manipulate him. She threatened to make sure her daughter knew the real truth about what rotten people they both were! Jim shared the letter with Barb, filed it away and went on with his business.

No reaction, no counter-rejection, no need to defend. Jim was free to parent his daughter to the best of his ability without responding to Mary's anger. Why? Jim had freed himself of emotional bondage, and Mary's guilt and expectations long ago. He'd asked forgiveness for failing as a husband and had gone on with his life.

What about Barb? It always hurts when someone continues to hate you, or falsely accuses you, but Barb, too, was emotionally free of Mary. Barb had the confidence of loving herself enough and having Jim's love and trust that she didn't need Mary to "like" her. Barb had also learned that trying to explain or defend herself to an emotionally closed person is a waste of time.

LEGAL RIGHTS CARRY THE MOST WEIGHT

Unfortunately, many of the natural rights we have as parents are taken away or restricted after divorce. Our level of control over family situations may drastically change. Careful planning of your divorce and visitation agreement is the key to maximizing the control you'll be able to retain after divorce.

Control is often just an illusion. If people respond the way we want, it's because they are making a choice to respond so.

When things seem to be getting out of control in our lives, it's important to remember that God is in ultimate control of our lives, and since He loves us and promises to care for us, this should be a comforting thought!

WHAT YOU CAN'T CONTROL

Following are some of the most frequently reported areas where divorced people battle for control. They are separated into those things you can and can't "control." While these guidelines are addressed to the noncustodial father, the same principles apply to both parents, custodial or noncustodial.

Anything that goes on in her home

Unless something is illegal, you have no control. Document and report to authorities any illegal actions or breaches of the divorce or visitation agreement. The courts will be better able to advise you in each state and county what your chances are

The Castle Walls

of enforcing certain behavior. Still, some things may not be enforceable.

Anything she says to the kids

Even if the court agreement says not to alienate the affections of children from the other parent, it happens frequently and cannot be practically enforced. Documentations of this type of "small" thing may only be helpful when they are submitted with greater violations of the agreement.

Anything she does with the kids

No matter where she goes, whom she visits or what they do, if it's not illegal, you can't control it.

Anything she gives the kids

If she gives them their own TV, phone, stereo at early ages, lets them watch *Beavis and Butthead* or eat too much candy, you can't control it.

What she lets the kids wear or how she dresses them

Where she takes the kids to get their hair cut, or the style. What clothes they wear, how often they bathe, brush their teeth at her house, or how early they go to bed. You have no control, even if what you want is "good" for them.

What doctor/counselor she decides to have the kids see

The doctor may be a quack and the counselor may be a nut; the only control you may have is if you have sufficient proof (documentation, witnesses, etc.) that they are being abused in some way. Then you still have a court battle ahead.

What church she or the kids attend

She has the freedom to choose the child's religion. So do you. Take advantage of your time with the kids and teach them as much as you can about your own faith.

Where she sends the kids to school

The kids may be in an average school and you may offer to pay full tuition for the best private school in town. She doesn't have to accept.

How she spends your child support

You see her new clothes and jewelry while the kids are still wearing the same old shoes. You can choose to buy them new shoes, but you can't deduct it from your child support, and you have no legal right to demand she reimburse you.

What companions she lets them play with

If she lets them play with children who are a bad influence, all you can do, and should do, is talk to your child about why you don't like them playing with those kids. Keep communication open and honest, even if you can't change the situation.

Where the kids sleep in her home

Lots of lonely, divorced mothers let their children sleep with them, even when they begin to get "too old." Keep communication open with the child on why they have their own bed at your house. It's a temptation for many mothers to "adultify" their little boys and they soon become Mom's "surrogate spouse." This is sometimes labeled as "emotional incest" and can be categorized as a form of child abuse. If mothers are still letting their boys climb into bed with them, you may want to seek the advice of a counselor to check out your options in stopping this.

What movies she takes them to/what books she lets them read

Noncustodial fathers have a bad reputation for letting their kids do whatever they want, but custodial mothers can be just as guilty of this overindulgence and permissiveness.

The Castle Walls

Whether or not she shows up on time at your home

You can't control what time she'll arrive to pick up or deliver the children, but you can do the driving yourself to retain more control.

WHAT YOU CAN CONTROL

Generally the only things you can control are situations when the children are in your physical custody. Some examples are:

What time the kids go to bed in your home.

What they eat, play and watch on TV in your home.

What they wear while they're with you.

Where they go and whom they're with (unless court orders prohibit).

Their discipline.

Their religious upbringing.

Their supplemental education or training, such as music lessons.

Where you go on vacation.

Your visits to the kids' schools.

Your communication with the teachers and other leaders.

Their allowance at your house.

How often they see your friends and relatives.

What toys they have in your home.

LET LIFE TEACH YOUR KIDS

Let the kids be late or miss an event due to their other parent's lack of consideration for your schedule. Allow the pressure from the children to fall on her, where it belongs. Children will observe and learn more about punctuality, schedules, common courtesy, communication and boundary setting than you could ever tell them in words. Kids will begin to realize they too don't have to suffer because of someone else's behavior and that they always have options.

DON'T PLAY THE MARTYR

You might be tempted to miss your party or other event just to show your ex-spouse how badly he/she messed up your life once again. That's bitterness.

You can't control how the ex-spouse will behave, but you can control how you respond to your ex-spouse.

Chapter 14

Being Willing to Lose in Order to Win

✥

om and I found ourselves, once again, in high-back chairs in the attorney's well-appointed office. As we waited for him to return from the copy machine, I surveyed the marble finish, plush carpet, wetbar and polished Russian saber hung over his desk. "Yep," I thought to myself, "no wonder attorney fees are so high!" Immediately, though, I knew I should be less judgmental of his polished saber and more grateful for his polished legal skills. More than once he'd come to our rescue in solving legal and visitation problems. Our attorney walked in carrying the usual large load of paperwork.

"Well, Tom and Rose, I have some good news and some bad news." I winced and rolled my eyes. Tom let out a sarcastic sigh, then asked, "What is it *this* time?"

"Your ex-wife is refusing to let you have any extra time in the summer with your son. She is also not happy with the visitation agreement and has some new scheduling demands. She's prepared to fight, and it seems she has unlimited funds. There may be professional psychological testing for everyone. On top of everything else, she's insisting that a third attorney be hired to represent the child, and you'll have to

The Castle Walls

pay those fees. To fight in court for that extra time, you're looking at a possible bill of close to $20,000 and maybe 6 months of testing, filing and waiting for hearing dates — all with no guarantee."

I gulped and tried to be funny, "What's the bad news?" Tom just sat there.

Because of my get-to-the-bottom-line personality, I thought, "Well that shuts the door on that!" knowing full well we didn't have $20,000 lying around to pay a professional to help us get to spend time with Tom's son in the summer. Although it made me angry and sad at the same time, I didn't want to deal with six more months of emotional battling. I needed to let go. Tom couldn't let go that quickly.

I looked over at my husband and saw the deep grief in his eyes. He loves his son so much, and has never been able to get any extra time with him without resistance, some condition or problem. I could tell he was angry, too, but that would come later. All I saw on his face was hurt and hopelessness.

When we went home that night, Tom began to get angry. He started planning how he could get his hands on $20,000. Part of me wanted to fight too. I knew we could cash in our life insurance policies, IRAs and run up our credit cards. I, too, desperately wanted Mike to be with us in the summer because I love him and knew how important it was for a ten-year-old boy to start spending close time with his father. As Mike's other parents, Tom and I both felt that devoting whatever time, energy and resources we had to his mental and emotional well-being in the adolescent years would be of prime importance.

We argued a little over the pros and cons, not really angry with each other, but with the situation. I changed my mind every ten minutes about what I thought we should do. Finally Tom and I sat down and did our "problem solving," using the techniques we'd learned in counseling. One of the most important principles which had freed us from bondage to people and things was the ability to "be willing to lose in order to win."

We agreed that getting more time with "our" son was of primary importance and considered it our duty to try everything we could to make it happen. However, we also took a realistic look at the price we'd pay:

+ We'd be in major debt for close to 7-10 years, or longer if the costs were greater than $20,000.
+ For years, we'd have no available credit for other major purchases or needs that might arise.
+ We'd be under constant stress without a financial cushion.
+ We'd have to pay penalties to cash our IRAs.
+ We'd have to wait years to start a retirement account again, losing interest we would have built up.
+ Costs of new insurance after our debts would be paid would be higher.
+ If one of us died, the other would not be financially protected.
+ We'd take the risk that if the truth got twisted in court, which does happen, we'd actually end up paying her costs, too, and might even lose our home.
+ We'd spend the next six months in a negative emotional "fight" mode trying to prove ourselves to the courts.
+ We'd be emotionally consumed with whether or not we won, in bondage to the outcome.
+ We'd be under constant character attack and prone to bitterness.
+ We'd have no guarantee that when all was said and done we would get any extra time with Mike.
+ We'd take the risk, as small as it seemed, that we might actually lose some of the time we did have with Mike if a judge was so inclined.
+ The stress, anger and fighting would put tremendous strain on Mike, who had already been put in the middle.
+ Mike would be asked his opinion by attorneys, psychologists and judges, under constant fear of rejection by one parent if he showed favoritism to another.

It was tempting to forge ahead with the fight anyway. It seemed a noble battle, and many people considered us the victims, rooting for our "side." How self-sacrificing to lose our financial security and possibly our home, all for the sweet, tender child who "needed" his father!

Wait a minute! Casting the melodrama aside, we took another look at the facts. Although our time with Mike was limited, we were able to see him several times a month and could call him on the phone. Tom had learned to make the most of his time with Mike and was able to talk to him, teach and guide him as fathers should, even in a several-hour period. Did we really need six extra weeks in the summer to prepare Mike for manhood, *or could we accomplish nearly the same effect by making sure we used our limited time wisely?*

Based on these facts, and because of Mike's still young age, we made the decision together to lose in order to win. We knew that when Mike was a little more mature, he would be able to speak more clearly about his needs and wants, and be emotionally able to make changes about where he lived or the length of visits. We would try again in a few years to review the situation, and meanwhile would begin to build a legal fund.

Tom conceded to the changes his ex-wife wanted in the visitation schedule, and dropped his request for additional time in the summer with his son. We grieved our lost hopes and began to focus on the time we *did* have with Mike. It was hard, and we had to be careful that our natural anger did not fester into bitterness at his ex-wife, her attorney, and even the court system. We lost the tug-of-war, but we won our emotional sanity, our financial security and protected Mike from emotional stress which he may not have been ready to handle.

Problem Solving

"Losing to Win" is a key principle in learning to solve problems with an ex-spouse or any other adversary. It should never be viewed as passive submission to conflict, or as playing "the martyr." It is a choice based on priorities. In any problem situation, there are many things we would like to happen, and many things we want to avoid. Of our options and the anticipated results, we need to choose the solution that *focuses on our highest priorities*. This technique works for ex-spouses, too.

In trying to find solutions to problems, husbands and wives should already have in mind, and even have written down, what their common goals and priorities will be. When we're lost in the confusion of emotional responses during conflict, a priority list comes in handy. Some suggested priorities could be:

To put my spouse's emotional needs (not wants) as top priority

To meet the children's emotional needs (not wants)

To stop assuming responsibility for the ex-spouse

To remain as fair as possible in our dealings with the ex-spouse

To never engage in battle in front of the children

PURPOSE OF OUR PROBLEMS

Problems are tools God uses to help us grow, not weapons to hurt us. We should develop an "attitude of gratitude" by thanking God each day for our trials. Troubles mean that God is tapping us on the shoulder and saying, "I have another character quality I want you to develop. Now don't forget to ask me for grace when the going gets tough, because I've got plenty to spare! I know you can do it!"

Now this is the last thing you want to hear when you're in the middle of an emotional response to the latest conflict, but if you can learn to look in the mirror each day and say "Thank you, God, for ALL my problems!" you will be on the road to real maturity. The new attitude of gratitude for your problems is one of the best weapons you can have in fighting any problem.

Look for the Positive Purpose. When we resist our problems, or hope they go away, they will only grow and come more rapidly. When we find this happening, we should stop and ask, "Okay, what character quality can I develop this time?" If we seek with an open mind and heart, the answer will come, as well as the necessary grace to work through it.

The Castle Walls

PARTNERS IN THE PROBLEM

We need to be "partners" with God in solving our problems. He opens doors; we pick up our legs and walk through. The four basic steps in problem solving are:

Admit the Problem

We shouldn't feel guilty because we have problems, everyone does! We shouldn't feel like a failure if we have problems, everyone fails!

Accept the Problem

The Serenity Prayer
Lord, grant me the serenity to accept the things I cannot change,
the courage to change the things I can,
and the wisdom to know the difference.

Appreciate the Problem

Write the words, "Thank you, God, for ALL my problems," and tape it to your bathroom mirror. Look in the mirror and thank Him until it becomes a daily habit. Paste a copy at work on your computer, in the car or other area where you spend most of your day. Recite it, think it, feel it!

Attack the Problem

First, determine the real cause(s) of the problem. Second, consider what potential growth for you is in this problem. Third, write down all the worst things that could happen as a result of this problem. Imagine as far as you can, even including death, bankruptcy, never seeing your children again, having her turn the children against you for life, losing their love, having your whole family disown you, etc. Address your *worst* fears.

Ask Yourself:
What do I really fear?
Why do I fear it?

Being Willing to Lose in Order to Win

Do I have all the facts, or am I jumping to conclusions?
What can I lose in this?
Will I survive these losses?
Is there someone I can talk to and get an objective view?

Fourth, reconcile yourself to accepting and surviving the worst! Imagine the worst has happened. Let yourself feel the hurt, agony or grief. Complete a "dress rehearsal" grieving process, from anger, guilt and grief, to acceptance, release and recovery. Imagine God with you, comforting you and saying, "Let go now. I will turn all this to good in my way, in my time. Trust me." Then let go.

Fifth, calmly and with trust, devote your time and energy into improving upon the worst. With a new attitude that you can lose it all and still "be okay," you'll be less anxious in working through options for change.

Use this checklist:

Who can help me with this problem?
What information, paperwork, details do I need to gather, copy, document or record to help solve the conflict?
What legal recourse do I have?
Is my spouse supportive of, or can he/she recommend any methods of "improving upon the worst?"
What books/tapes/resources are available to help this situation?

"Sometimes God calms the storm.
Sometimes He lets the storm rage while He calms His child."
Gary Lawrence, *Mental Morsels* (self-published, 1992), p. 25.

♥ ♥ ♥

"And we know that in all things God works for the good of those who love him, who have been called according to his purpose."
Romans 8:28

Chapter 15

How to Win on the Phone: Twelve Telephone Tips

✥

One of the most common times that arguments with an ex-spouse ensue is on the telephone. You're aware by now that you'll never be able to completely avoid conflict with the ex-spouse, but you can learn how to respond in a healthy way. The twelve tips which follow will help you avoid "losing it" on the phone. Believe me, these practical responses work!

1. ROLE PLAY

This can actually be fun, help you vent frustration, ease tension and gain confidence before you have to talk to your ex-spouse. You play the part of yourself; have your new spouse or a friend play the "ex." Now pretend you've dialed the number and your "ex" has picked up the phone. Have your partner respond in all the worst ways you can imagine. Begin with the response your ex-spouse actually gave the last time you argued on the phone. Now, using the rest of the techniques which follow, start practicing the better way to communicate.

The Castle Walls

2. REFUSE THE GUILT

When your ex-spouse falsely accuses you during a conversation, or attacks your character, learn to respond with "I refuse to receive that false guilt." Memorize it. Don't be snotty about it, and never say it in anger. If you feel the anger rising, go immediately to tip No. 9. If you find yourself repeating this more than three times, try "The Bottom Line" (No. 4) or go to No. 10, the "Nonviolent Hang-up."

3. MAGIC MIRROR

One of the most frustrating elements of communication is when we feel the other person just doesn't hear us or misunderstands what we are saying. Not only is it good communication, but it's an act of love and concern for another to learn to mirror their comments or feelings: repeat back to them a condensed version of what you think they said.

Let's say your ex-spouse just blasted you for being irresponsible and doesn't want you to pick up the kids from school. Instead, he/she'll drive them to your house when he/she feels like it. Using the mirroring technique, a good response might be: "What I heard was you are afraid I won't pick the kids up from school on time and you're worried they will be stranded without a ride. Is that correct?" If you're wrong, allow the other person to correct you. If you heard correctly, you can then proceed with working out a solution. Your spouse will be much more likely to work with you after feeling that you took a minute to HEAR him/her.

4. BUY SOME TIME

When your ex-spouse makes a demand or asks for a commitment of your time, attention or money, get in the habit of *not responding immediately*. Time is a wonderful gift you can give yourself. Learn to mirror your spouse's feelings and say, "I hear your concerns and requests, and I need until (tomorrow, this weekend, etc.) to get back to you with my answer." This allows you time to process without anger, to check your calendar, your financial situation and to seek the counsel of your mate as to other schedules, plans or needs. If your ex-spouse ridicules you for not being able to answer right away, or demands an immediate answer, just ignore those comments. *You're being smart!*

5. THE BOTTOM LINE

When your "ex" is snotty, giving excuses, beating around the bush or going off on a tangent, bring the conversation back to the bottom line. "So, will you let us have the kids Saturday or not?" If the answer is no, accept it. Unless there are other matters to discuss, close the conversation. If you want to ask again, or have your request reconsidered, do it in a letter. She/he probably won't give you the satisfaction of a "yes" during this conversation, but time may work on her/him. Again, it may not. Be prepared to accept her/his answer. You may have to repeat the "bottom line" question a few times until she/he answers. If you find yourself repeating the bottom line like a broken record, ask for another time when you will be able to get an answer and end the conversation.

6. AVOID THE BROKEN RECORD

Are you hearing yourself explaining the same thing you just explained over and over just a few minutes ago? Your ex-spouse probably does hear what you say the first time you say it. You are probably getting yourself worked up, and giving your ex-spouse power, by repeating it over and over. Get smart! Get to the "Bottom Line" or end the conversation using No. 10.

7. DON'T "DEXTIFY"

Don't waste your energy unnecessarily Defending, EX-plaining or tesTIFYing yourself to her. Concentrate instead on what your ex-spouse is trying to tell you. Communicate facts or information, stick with what it is you called for and get on with the conversation. You owe your ex-spouse honest, clear communication, but not excuses.

8. TAKE YOUR TEMPERATURE

Do you hear your voice start to rise? Are you clenching the phone or having shortness of breath? Learn to tune in to your own body signals that a blowout might be right around the corner. You may not be the personality type to yell or scream, but even soft-spoken people can get sarcastic and say things that hurt, things they'll regret. The minute you feel yourself lose even a little of your calmness, try getting back to the "bottom line" or use the Nonviolent Hang-up, #10, below.

9. ASK FOR A LETTER

When the conversation is confusing, heated and getting nowhere fast, a very reasonable request is to say, "I'd like to consider everything you're saying, and it would help me if you'd write it all down in a letter. As soon as I get it, I'll get back to you within a day or two at the latest." There's no sense going over and over little details when one or both of you are irritated or emotional. Make sure you keep your commitment and get back to the other person as soon as you can, and never purposely keep her/him waiting for your reply. A letter also gives you a permanent record of what was said or requested. If the other person refuses, let her/him know you're not able to continue communicating on the phone (NOT because of her/him) because (now this is where you take ownership of your own responses) you have a hard time on the phone and aren't able to give the time and attention that her/his thoughts deserve, for the kids sake! There's nothing unmanly or wimpy about wanting to avoid phone fights.

10. Nonviolent Hang-up (Grown-up's Version of "Time-Out")

If all else fails, or your ex-spouse is getting nasty, quickly and firmly interrupt and say, "I'm sorry, but I have to hang up. Please either send me a letter or call me later." Don't wait to hear a reply — hang up! Do what you said you're going to do. Never use this in anger, or as a punishment, and don't slam the phone down. If your "ex" was shouting and probably didn't hear you, go ahead and repeat it once, but then hang up. If you tell someone two or three times you're going to do something and don't do it, you lose credibility.

11. Don't Call Back When the Other Person Hangs Up

If he/she just hung up on you, he/she "took control" of the situation. You may feel helpless, angry or obliged to call back and continue. His/her emotional level is obviously high right now. Don't call back. Your "ex" can refuse to pick up, which will frustrate you even more. Wait until emotional levels are down.

12. Post These Rules

Copy, reduce or otherwise duplicate these tips and keep them posted by all your phones. When this book is laying out on the coffee table or in your car, it won't be any help when the phone rings and the person to whom you were once married is waiting to talk to you!

These tips are also very helpful when you're speaking in person. They're harder to recall unless you memorize or practice them with a partner. When you're having a face-to-face conversation, instead of the nonviolent hang-up, just physically leave, though never in a huff. *Don't forget that deep breath!*

*I also recommend the book, *The Verbally Abusive Relationship* by Patricia Evans (Holbrook, MA: Adams Media, 1996).

Chapter 16

How to Win in a Letter

◆━◆✟◆━◆

riting allows you to get your emotions down on paper before you say anything you'd regret later. It helps clear your mind and organize your thoughts. If you choose to write, express only the "what and why" of your concerns. If you are setting boundaries, make sure they are clear and that your ex-spouse knows what consequences will occur. Be specific with dates and times.

A letter is also a powerful written testimony to your beliefs, desire to stand up for what's right for you, your mate and your children, and your effort to communicate. Your ex-spouse can and probably will show your letter to outside parties, including friends, family members and the court. When you're willing to "go on record," you make a strong stand as head of your family.

OTHER BENEFITS OF LETTERS

✦ Letters help prevent potential face-to-face confrontations.
✦ Letters allow the recipient to digest the contents at his/her own pace, in his/her own space.

The Castle Walls

✦ If he/she refuses to take your phone calls or unplugs the answering machine, you can still communicate with a letter.

Here are two sample letters, one written before incorporating the previous suggestions, one after. Which do you think is best?

Letter No. 1

Dear ex-wife:

I can't believe how you never let the kids call me. Every time I call, you tell me they're busy and you'll have them call back, but they never do. The court agreement says I have the right to call them until 8:00 p.m. You are deliberately trying to keep me out of the kids lives! You'd better start complying with the court orders, or believe me, you'll suffer the consequences! I want you to have them call me every Tuesday and Thursday night at 7:00 p.m. so I can talk to them. When you don't let me talk to them, you are only hurting them!

Your ex-husband

Letter No. 2

Dear ex-wife:

I'd like to be able to talk to the kids more, and I have some suggestions. Please let me know by next weekend what you think would work for you:

– Have them call me Tues. and Thurs. nights between 7-8 PM.

– Let me know two other days or times during the week, after 6 PM that would be better for you.

– Allow me to install a phone in the kids' room that is just for them to talk to me. That way I can call without bothering you. I'll cover all costs.

I'm sure you understand the intent of the court order and I appreciate your working with me on this. If we can't work something out, I will call the court to help us resolve the issue.

Your ex-husband

Notice how all the "you did this, you did that" is deleted. The focus is not on the ex-wife's actions, but on the husband and what he wants. There are no threats, and he's given her some options to show his willingness to compromise. Compromise doesn't mean giving in, it means giving other choices a chance.

CONFIRM THE TRUTH

If your ex-spouse has made any statement with which you can agree, find it. One of the best ways to help lower the adversary's defenses is to honestly give credit and confirmation to their thoughts or ideas. If your ex-spouse tries to shame you by declaring "You need COUNSELING!" agree with him or her. "You're right" are sweet words to anyone's ear. She's right; sometimes you probably do need counseling just like the rest of us on earth. So what? If she says, "You're a rotten parent," you could respond with something like "I can always use some pointers in parenting." You didn't agree that you were rotten, but you did find some element of truth which can be confirmed. While this type of response doesn't guarantee an improved response, it often helps.

CLEAN IT UP

Never use a letter to attack. After you've written the letter, pretend the judge is reading it in court. Gives you a different perspective, doesn't it? Remove anything hostile or derogatory. The letter should only inform her of your concerns, plans and intentions. Use "I" statements instead of the accusatory "You" statements. Don't tell her what to do. Instead, inform her politely of what you'd like her to do and give her some options. Don't forget common courtesy words like please and thank you. Don't, however, try to manipulate her emotions by false niceties. Be honest and straightforward.

CHANGE THE PARTS WHERE YOU ASK HER TO CHANGE HER BEHAVIOR

One common problem we all have is that we tend to ask people to meet our needs, and when they don't, we try harder to threaten, force, shame, manipulate or otherwise control their behavior. Check your letter. Are you wasting time asking for something you are pretty sure she won't or doesn't legally have to give? Use the letter more for communicating what you will do or how you will respond to certain situations. Otherwise you're just setting yourself up to be victimized. Do you unconsciously think it makes her look bad and you look good? Don't play those games. If you find yourself in this situation, it may be time to seek forgiveness for your bitterness again!

SET SPECIFIC BOUNDARIES WITH DATES, TIMES AND CONSEQUENCES

When you leave open-ended requests ("please get back to me"), the chance of her not responding at all increases. When she doesn't respond, it leaves you uncertain or unable to finalize your own plans. It's a setup for bitterness. If you're asking for her to make a decision, set the time you'd like her to call or get back to you. "Please call me by this Friday or I will go ahead and sign him up for swimming lessons myself on Saturday." Be clear about the consequence of her response or lack or response. Letting her know what the consequences will be doesn't have to be a threat, just a clear communication of your intent. If she interprets it as a threat, respect her right to respond in her own capacity, but don't react to her response.

GET YOUR WIFE'S COUNSEL

Your wife, although she may be equally concerned or angry about a situation with the ex-wife, will feel secure knowing you are standing up for and protecting the children or your own personal or family boundaries by writing the letter. With that security, her anxiety level is likely to be lower than yours. With a softened heart, she should be a good source of rational, rather than emotional, input. Other benefits of sharing with your wife are these:

✦ the positive emotional bonding when two people work on a problem together

✦ an increase in your wife's trust that you will take care of future problems in a rational manner

✦ your wife's positive response to you as you honor her insight

KEEP A COPY

Battles in court often rely on written documentation. Maintaining files will help keep facts straight and help the court in making fair decisions. When it's "her word against yours," proof of written communication, dates and times will often make or break the case. If you are writing about a matter which may end up in front of the judge, send the letter *Certified, Return Receipt Requested* as proof she received it.

There's no preventing divorce from hurting children. When your kids reach adulthood, they'll tend to look back and question their parents' actions and motivations, especially if one parent has lied to the children about the other. Kids also grow up with distorted interpretations of what really happened in their youth. Consider, not for your own defense, but for the adult child's understanding, sharing some of your letters in future years. When you're asked the question, "Dad, why didn't you ever try to spend more time with me?" you can share the letter you wrote years before asking for that exta time, although it may have been denied. Often just the reassurance that you *tried* to make things right, whether they happened or not, can be an invaluable gift to your adult child.

CAST OFF HER ABUSIVE LETTERS

If she writes back, and her letters become abusive, refuse them by writing "refused, return to sender" on the outside and remail. Follow up with a call or note that you'll be glad to receive her letters when they are not abusive and stick only to the facts.

The Castle Walls

If she sends her letters certified or some other special delivery where you are constantly running back and forth to the post office, you may also refuse these letters. Follow up with a note or phone call that you'll accept regular mail or hand delivery, but don't have time to waste on extra trips to the mailbox. If she wants proof of delivery to you, she can hire a process server or deliver it herself. This puts the cost and inconvenience back on her. *Don't use the "refuse" to purposely anger, attack or inconvenience her.*

CONSIDER THE LILIES

God promises to help us in all things. There's a genuine physical release when, after we do everything in our power to solve a problem, we turn to our Heavenly Father and lay the burden at His feet. Pray for the kids, your ex-wife and your new wife.

A word of caution: don't pray that God will change your ex-wife to the way you think she should be. That's your will. He may have a greater plan you know nothing about. He is working in her life in ways you don't know, on a timetable unlike yours. Pray instead that:

+ her heart will ultimately be opened to His will
+ He send you the grace to respond to her the way you should
+ any hurts, mental, physical or emotional, to the kids be healed in His time, and that those hurts ultimately work toward good
+ your children's hearts will be open to Him despite the problems of divorce
+ the Holy Spirit will lead you as father and husband to all your children and your new wife

CRUISE!

Do the best in your written communications with an ex-spouse, but then let go! All of these steps are applicable when the ex-wife is dealing with an unreasonable or abusive ex-husband, too! Active personalities turn the steering wheel over to God and then jump back in His lap and grab the wheel. Passive personalities stay in the passenger seat but stare anxiously out the window and worry, worry, worry. What a lack of faith for both!

If we believe God's promises, and acknowledge His omnipotence, then why are we still hanging onto the problem? Let go and enjoy your blessings.

Chapter 17

The Visitation Agreement

⬥✟⬥

ancy picked her stepdaughter, Kelly, up after school on Friday for their weekend visitation. They drove to the city park where Kelly was going to play soccer with her team. When they got there, Kelly's mother, Anna, was at the playing field.

Anna hated her ex-husband's new wife. From the first day she had treated her as if she didn't exist and refused to call her by name. Over the years the bitterness toward Nancy had escalated to the point where Anna had threatened to kill Nancy. Anna was angry that Nancy had her husband, and jealous that her daughter had developed a deep love for her stepmom. In the beginning, Nancy had tried being friendly, but eventually learned that the best response was to keep a safe distance.

"If you're ever anywhere without me, honey, and you run into her, please get up and leave," Dave had instructed his wife.

"What if Kelly's with me?" Nancy asked her husband.

"Just take her and leave. Believe me, it's the best thing to do."

When Nancy saw Anna, she quietly asked her to leave. Nancy didn't realize that she had no right to ask Anna to leave

The Castle Walls

a public place, but did have full rights to control her own behavior. When Anna started yelling at her, Nancy quickly told the coach she had to leave and took Kelly with her. Anna ran after them and grabbed Kelly out of Nancy's grasp, returning to the ballfield. Nancy let go and didn't argue. She didn't want her stepdaughter torn in half.

Nancy called the sheriff, who asked to see her visitation agreement. Nancy pulled it from her purse, where she kept a signed copy. She also presented the officer with a signed letter from her husband authorizing her to have custody of his children during his visitation time if he was at work or on a call. The sheriff agreed that Nancy, not Kelly's mother, had legal custody at that moment. He brought Kelly back to Nancy, and they left the park.

WHO'S IN CONTROL?

The visitation agreement is a fully enforceable, legal document which grants the control of the children to the parent with scheduled visitation. For the majority of noncustodial parents, visitation rights are complete. During the visits, the custodial parent has no legal authority over where the visiting parent goes, what they do, what they say or whom they're with.

This is emotionally difficult for the parent who is normally in control of their child. When a parent is used to being "in charge" all the time, it's hard to let go and let the child go into the home or environment of an ex-spouse and other people who may be strangers to the custodial parent.

It's important for visiting parents to realize the extent of their rights and enjoy the freedom from control by the other parent. Sometimes this is the only opportunity to teach the children or expose them to situations which are normally not available to them at the other parent's home. Some children only get to attend church services when they are on alternate weekend visits. Some only get to play with their cousins or visit other relatives when they visit on alternate weekends.

This freedom can be guaranteed or denied depending on the structure of the visitation agreement.

Noncustodial parents who don't have a clearly spelled out visitation agreement are subject to the emotional whims of the custodial parent. If you don't have it in writing with the judge's signature, legally, there is nothing you can do about it. Sometimes, in mediation sessions, parents may agree to a change in the written agreement. Because it takes up the court's time and costs legal and filing fees, many mediators will recommend both parties "jot down" the agreed changes and have an "understanding" about the new changes, rather than go back to court. Don't let the mediator talk you into handwriting changes into the agreement! If either party decides they don't agree to the change, and it wasn't formally filed with the judge, the agreement reverts to the original typed instructions. Police or sheriffs cannot enforce handwritten changes. To avoid the greatest number of potential problems, these four steps will help parents construct a workable visitation agreement.

ANTICIPATE

Sit down with a regular calendar and the kids' school calendar. Bring your work calendar home, too. Start at the beginning of the year and go through each weekend, holiday and birthday, anticipating how you would like the visitation to go. Anticipate any problems you may foresee. Do you think he'll deliberately plan vacations where you'll miss Mother's Day? Be prepared. Follow the guidelines in this chapter.

ARTICULATE

Draw up a clear and concise list of your desires for visitation dates, times, transportation arrangements. Some attorneys will try to talk you out of a lengthy or detailed visitation agreement. They might not think it's necessary, and they may charge you more for it. The extra time and money is not an expense to the attorney, it's an investment in your future peace. Your

The Castle Walls

attorney doesn't have to live with the consequences of an ex-wife not showing up on time or refusing to let you have your child on Father's Day! The more detailed the agreement, the less opportunity for misinterpretation or argument.

ALTERNATE

Anticipate any objections or demands the other parent may voice, and have an alternate plan ready for negotiation. If you can't agree who will get Christmas Day or the child's birthday, alternating is always a good way to go.

ARBITRATE

Once you have a written agreement in place, be willing to trade and work with an ex-spouse regarding visitation times and dates. If you both agree the child can stay an hour or day, you don't have to stick with the letter of the agreement. If you can't agree, you'll have the written agreement to fall back on.

Always carry a CERTIFIED copy of the court agreement, with all parties' signatures, including the judge's, in all family cars, at work, at home. Many law enforcement officers won't accept a xerographic copy. You never know when you'll need to make quick reference in confirming plans or schedules with other parties (travel agents, teachers, baby-sitters).

When you need the assistance of a law enforcement officer to help you get custody of the children, you'll also need to produce a signed copy of the visitation agreement.

Whether you already have an agreement in place, or need to go back to court to modify it, here are some of the important things to consider in your visitation agreement:

Weekends

Most divorced parents in the same town or within proximity alternate weekend visits with their children. The time between "every other weekend" can be a very long time not to see your children if you are the noncustodial parent, and an equally long time for them not to have you in their lives. Most fathers who live in the same town also get one visitation day in the middle of the week, from after school to after dinner. You'll want to pick the children up early enough on weekends to enjoy Friday night, and keep them long enough to enjoy a full Sunday. The courts usually recommend the children return in time to "get ready for school the next day." For younger children the return time is usually 6:00 p.m. For older kids, times usually range from 6:00 - 8:00 p.m.

Pick-up Times

Be careful about setting this time in the visitation agreement. For weekend visits, you may assume Fridays will be school days, but sometimes they're not. If you agree to 6:00 p.m. pickup times, but the kids are off one Friday and you'd love to leave town early for a weekend at the beach, the custodial parent can prevent you from leaving early if he/she wants.

A better solution is to agree to "at the end of school on Friday." For parents who work and can't always get to a child right after school, "anytime between the end of school on Friday and the close of the day care center, which is 6:00 p.m."

If Friday is a holiday and the child is at home with his/her custodial parent or at day care, "anytime after 9:00 a.m. if the first day of the weekend is a nonschool day." This allows the visiting parent to get in a longer weekend if he/she can get off work.

Who Provides Transportation

Many parents split the transportation, with Mom dropping off and Dad taking home. For all parents involved, the advantage is they only have to drive one time. The disadvantage is having your plans disrupted or even ruined if he shows up late. What if she doesn't show up at all? It might be wise to do all the picking up and dropping off, as it affords you more control over the situation when you can't rely on an ex-spouse.

The Castle Walls

Donna sometimes didn't show up at the end of the week-end to pick up her son. She'd call at the last minute and say, "I'm sick," "I'm really tired," or "The car broke down." Brian ended up driving the one-and-a-half hour trip to her house both at the beginning and end of most weekend visits.

Brian made a deal with his ex-wife Donna. "Whoever wants, gets." If Brian wanted to see his son for the weekend, he went and picked him up. If Donna wanted her son back home at the end of the weekend, she went to get him. If she didn't make arrangements to come pick him up, Brian had him spend the night or miss school until Donna came to get him. It worked.

Who Picks Up the Children

Many times stepparents need to pick up the kids from school for the weekend visitation. The visitation should clearly spell out who is permitted to pick the children up in the absence of their birth parent. New husbands or wives should have full authority, through their mate's parental rights, to transport the children whether the mate is custodial or non-custodial. It's a good idea to check with your attorney, though, as some fathers do not have "joint legal custody" and there may be restrictions that apply. In most cases where the father has joint legal custody, he has equal control over the "health, education, and welfare" of his children, even though they do not live with him full time. This authority may be passed through him to an adult of his choice.

If you're the new spouse of the noncustodial parent, carry a note in your wallet at all times that is signed by your mate:

My wife [husband],_____(name) has my permission to provide nonemergency or emergency medical care or other-wise provide for the health, welfare or education, including transportation of my children _____(names), during the times they are in her [his] physical custody.

Signed (parent's name, address and telephone number)

Where Will They Pick Up the Children

If the pickup place is to be different than the children's homes or schools, make sure other locations are "mutually agreed upon." This prevents unfair mileage and time requirements for either parent.

HOLIDAYS

Holidays are a special time with kids, and visitations are usually not very fair for the noncustodial parent. Don't try to split Thanksgiving. Alternate every year. School holidays which fall on Mondays should go with the parent who has that weekened. Some years it may seem one parent always gets Memorial or Labor Day, but over time (a seven-year period) it evens out. Make sure the visitation agreement states what time the children are picked up and returned on holidays.

Fireworks on July 4th usually don't start until about 9:00 p.m. If the normal return time for a holiday is earlier, put it in the agreement that July 4th extends to 10:00 p.m. or other agreed upon time.

Birthdays

Let the kids be with Mom on her birthday, with Dad on his. Alternate the child's visits on their birthdays every year. Don't try to compete by throwing two birthday parties. The ex-spouse may invite some or all the children you were planning to have over, and he/she will schedule hers a few days before you. You may want to get the kid a favorite movie or cartoon theme birthday cake, and she'll beat you to it. Let go. Let your "ex" give the party one year. You give it the next. Another option is just to let him/her host and pay for all the parties all the time, every year. Noncustodial parents can schedule a family dinner with cake and enjoy an intimate celebration as an alternate. Kids don't need two birthday parties.

The Castle Walls

Easter

Easter can be alternated every year, and should include any school vacation time that accompanies the holiday. Some parents who want to give their younger children Easter baskets try to tell them the bunny came to both houses. Same with Santa. We found the best approach for the children is to let the other parent get the Easter basket or Santa presents on his/her scheduled years, and let go of trying to compete if it's not "our" year. The next year we do Bunny and Santa "duty." It's preferable to share this approach with the ex-spouse and ask for his/her cooperation. Be prepared for a refusal, however, and let go.

Thanksgiving

For parents who travel, it's good to have the Wednesday before Thanksgiving to allow time to arrive. The holiday visitation should begin after school on Wednesday, or at least some time Wednesday night. If a father's midweek visitation day is Wednesday, he should forfeit the day for the ex-wife during her years on Thanksgiving, *if she has to travel a long way.* The ex-wives may give him an extra day in exchange.

Mother's Day

Even if it's Dad's weekend, the children's mother should get this day with her children, if she wants. Some mothers, when the children are very small, may just want a day for themselves! Many agreements are from 8:00 a.m. to 8:00 p.m. that day.

Dads, plan a special day or evening just before Mother's Day to have you and her stepchildren give *your wife* Mother's Day presents, cards or some other special remembrance. Treat her the same as if she was their birth mother. Honor her role as another parent and encourage your children to honor her too!

Father's Day

Even if it's her weekend, she needs to let the ex-husband have the children, if he wants them. She should not plan any vacations during June that would result in having the children away from their Dad on Father's Day. Anticipate her vacation plans. Ask ahead of time.

Mothers, plan a special day just before Father's Day to have you and his stepchildren give *your* husband Father's Day presents, cards, etc. Treat him the same as if he was their birth father. Honor his role as another parent and encourage your children to honor him too!

Christmas

Don't ruin your Christmas day trying to split it up! Every family I've talked to who tried to split Christmas day in half was unhappy with the arrangement. It's too hard on Christmas day to pack up at noon and drive the kids to the other parent's, or put them on a plane or train. The best solution is splitting the Christmas vacation "in half" up to the day *after* Christmas. This way, each parent gets a full, uninterrupted Christmas day with the kids every other year. Be willing to lose this one in order to truly win. Because of the school schedules, each year one parent will get more time and it won't be a "fair" split. The next year, however, that parent gets more time. Over the years it will even out.

Make sure that alternate weekend visits don't cut into or interfere with the two-week Christmas vacation. Check to see that the visitation agreement clearly spells out that the first weekend of the two-week period goes with the parent who has the first half of the holiday time.

Make sure that all airplane reservations and other travel arrangements are made well in advance. Request that your ex-spouse get the air schedule confirmed at least 30 days in advance. This helps alleviate last minute disappointments. Ask for a copy of the itinerary from the travel agent to confirm that the reservations have actually been made. Talk to your attorney a few months ahead of time and be prepared with some alternate plans of action should there be any problem.

Summer

For kids who are off school three months during the summer, there are many possibilities, from splitting the vacation in half, to alternating time on a biweekly basis.

For kids who go to "year round" school, where there are three months on and one month off, parents usually split the four-week "off track" period with each having two straight weeks and forfeiting alternate weekends. Another schedule some parents have is for parents to alternate the 30-day "off" period when the kids are younger. When the children get older, they can spend every off-track period with the noncustodial parent, with the other parent visiting on alternate weekends.

Vacations

Everyone pretty much agrees that a vacation should last at least one week. Most families leave on a weekend and return some time during the next weekend. This means the parent with alternating weekend visitation is likely to lose a weekend. It's not fair to expect a vacationing family to return Friday, especially from a long distance, so the other parent can have their regularly scheduled weekend. The court mediators usually encourage this arrangement. What's "fair" about this is that it will work both ways.

Does your ex-spouse need your hotel room number when you're on vacation? No. She/he should, however, have the name and telephone number of the hotel operator to leave messages in case of emergency.

Does she/he need to know every detail of your itinerary? No. If you switch hotels, though, do communicate the name, location and main hotel telephone number. If you leave the country, provide copies of the *general* itinerary and visas or passports. *Some travel agents will require the custodial parent's permission or signature.*

WHEN THE CUSTODIAL PARENT SAYS THE KIDS ARE SICK OR DON'T WANT TO COME

For mild sickness, noncustodial parents can, and often want to, provide for the sick child(ren) in their home for the weekend anyway. Discuss this with the mediator or attorneys when drawing up agreements.

Some custodial parents try to control the visitation by advising their ex-spouses the kids don't "feel" like coming for their scheduled visit. Whether they feel like it or not, they are under the same legal obligation as their parents to follow the visitation schedule, barring extreme sickness. The custodial parent and the children are in "contempt of court" when they do not follow the court visitation orders. Care should be taken by the noncustodial parent in these situations. The child(ren) may need counseling or other professional help.

HEALTH, SAFETY AND MORALS

This is a "generic" paragraph that most agreements will contain and prohibits any behavior on either parent's part which would be detrimental to the child's physical or emotional well being. Although open to wide interpretation, and difficult to enforce, this is nonetheless a good "blanket" to include in the agreement.

RELOCATION

The agreement should always contain a clause that prohibits either parent from moving the child out of state (except for trips, vacations) permanently or for extended periods. Both parties should check the latest court rulings in their own state about change of custody when a parent moves and wants to take the child with them. The rules vary and depend on certain specific situations.

The Castle Walls

WHEN YOU HAVE TO CALL THE COPS

Most visitation parameters are included within the broader scope of other court mandates such as a "custody order." While there can be numerous recitations, these agreements most commonly include orders to both parties to:

avoid excessive use of alcoholic beverages while parenting the child

refrain from doing or permitting any third party to do anything that would be detrimental to the health, safety, morals and welfare of the child(ren)

avoid saying or doing anything that would tend to alienate the affection of the child(ren) from the other parent

avoid any harassment, annoyance or molestation of the other party (parent)

inform each other of new addresses and telephone numbers

OTHER ITEMS IN THE AGREEMENT

Frequently "extras" like braces, college, camp or sports are discussed. These items are very sensitive to the future financial situation of each parent and the child's personal circumstances. Rather than try to predict all future plans, it's often best to wait to discuss these issues as they arise. The child support payment should already include "extras" such as typical music or sports programs, yearbooks, special school trips and the like. Be careful of locking yourself into "big ticket" items that you won't be able to afford later.

VIOLATING THE ORDER

The visitation agreement is a legally binding court order, and violation of the order results in being in contempt of court. Consequences of being in contempt can include jail time and fines. If you find yourself the victim of the other parent consistently violating the agreement (late pickup, no shows, verbal abuse, telephone harassment, etc.), you are encouraged by the courts to file complaints when necessary and to call the sheriff or other officer of the law to assist you.

If the custodial parent won't let the noncustodial parent have the child(ren) because of nonpayment of child support, the custodial parent is in contempt of court. The sheriff can accompany you as the noncustodial parent to the place where you think the children are located and remove them from the other parent's custody and place them into yours. The officer is there to enforce the court order and "keep the peace," not to intimidate or punish the other parent.

In most states, *vistation* and *child support are separate issues,* and a custodial parent has no right to refuse visitation to a parent who has not paid child support. This certainly is not "fair" when the "deadbeat dads" refuse to support their children but want to take them for a weekend of fun. Until the legal systems get tougher on these fathers, mothers will have to suffer.

Unfortunately, many angry, hurt and bitter ex-spouses will refuse visitation for a myriad of other reasons: he wasn't nice to her on the phone or she takes them to a church he doesn't like. None of these are valid reasons for violating the court order.

Calling the cops will make the uncooperative parent angry, but it can send a powerful messsage to both her/him and the children that you mean what you say and are willing to back up your rights with whatever legal means it takes. This action can also teach the kids how to set and enforce their own boundaries.

Part III

The Royal Treatment

*"There is no more lovely, friendly and charming
relationship, communion or company
than a good marriage."*

Martin Luther

Chapter 18

Your Personalities

W hen I started getting to know my husband's ex-wife, I began to realize that in many ways, *I was just like her!* Agggh-h-h-h! How could that be? I already knew the answer. I'd just finished reading popular Christian author Florence Littauer's best-selling book, *Personality Plus* (Old Tappan, NJ: Revell, 1983). I'd picked it up in an effort to find out why my husband's temperament seemed to be so opposite of mine. While I was assertive, he tended to be more "laid back." I liked to take charge of situations, and he liked to wait and see what happened first. He has more of a serious nature, while I like to tease and have fun. I thought if I could figure him out, our marriage would improve. Thanks to *Personality Plus*, we both learned why we did the things we did, and we began to view each other with a new understanding and appreciation!

Personality Plus taught us that each of us is born with a God-given personality. Even as babies we either cried and demanded our rights, or laid there and cooed. The following descriptions are of the four basic personalities that were originally identified and named by Hippocrates, hundreds of years before Christ was born. Today, many types of personality and

The Royal Treatment

temperament tests are all based in part on these original four personalities.

The *"Popular" Sanguines* love to have fun. They are bright and cheerful in their attitude and are usually the life of the party. They are clever, creative and love to tell stories. They love people and people usually love to be around them.

The *"Powerful" Cholerics* are the natural born leaders. They like to take charge and usually do a good job of seeing the big picture and getting the job done. They like challenges and are tireless workers. As leaders, Cholerics like to be appreciated for all their efforts.

The *"Perfect" Melancholies* are the world's geniuses. They are creative, introspective, deep and analytical. Melancholies love details and strive for perfection. They need to know that others understand them and will be sensitive to them.

The *"Peaceful" Phlegmatics* are well-balanced, consistent and easy-going. They are sympathetic, kind and are good, steady workers. Filled with compassion and concern, they are rarely offensive to others. Phlegmatics get along with everyone, and everyone gets along with them.

OPPOSITES TEND TO MARRY

The Sanguine and Melancholy are opposites. Sanguines have a positive attitude toward life, while Melancholies realize that life is never perfect, and tend to have a negative outlook. Both have strengths; both have weaknesses. Neither is better, just different. The aggressive Cholerics are opposite of the passive Phlegmatics. Cholerics like to lead. Phlegmatics like to follow.

Because people are usually attracted to what is different and unique from themselves, opposites truly attract. When opposite personalities marry, they have the potential for filling each others' gaps, forming a balanced relationship. The trouble starts when our strengths, carried to extremes, become weaknesses.

I began to understand why my husband's ex-wife and I were alike. We are both Choleric and have a tendency to take charge. That is a strength my Phlegmatic husband was attract-ed to in *both* of us. Since we tend to have an affinity with those whose personality we share, understanding the personalities helped me to change my attitude about my husband's ex-wife. I remind myself we are two Choleric "sisters." If I love the per-sonality God gave me, how can I dislike it in her? I can't.

EACH OF US IS A BLEND

We are usually a blend of two of the personalities. The rea-son we don't have a "third" blend is that it would be opposite of one of the first two. We can't oppose ourselves. We can't have a cheerful, optimistic attitude toward life (Sanguine) and a natural tendency toward pessimism and negativity (Melancholy) at the same time. We're naturally either one or the other. We aren't born natural leaders (Choleric) who thrive on taking charge and simultaneously unassertive (Phlegmatic).

Cholerics can learn to "behave" in a quiet manner, but it doesn't come naturally to them. Phlegmatics can "learn" to lead a group of people, but they have a harder time than Cholerics. Sanguines can "learn" to be more serious about life, and Melancholies can "learn" to look at the bright side. To achieve balance, all of us can make a conscious effort to devel-op the strengths of the other personalities.

My Phlegmatic/Melancholy husband is peaceful and happy to let others be in charge. I, on the other hand, am Choleric/Sanguine, like to be in charge and am happy to let others fol-low! We've learned that for a happy marriage, or in any healthy relationship, we have to be careful that we don't carry these strengths to extremes.

STRENGTHS CARRIED TO EXTREMES

Weaknesses are not separate from strengths. Rather weak-nesses are strengths carried to extremes. If left uncontrolled, weaknesses become compulsions, which manifest themselves as addictions.

The Royal Treatment

Have you ever known a *Sanguine* personality, the bubbly, talkative type? They start to grate on your nerves when they never stop talking to let you get a word in, or when they exaggerate their stories to the point of lying. Their natural strength for colorful storytelling becomes a weakness. Why? They are "Rejection Junkies."

When *Sanguines* fear rejection, they try even harder to get people to notice and like them. They will talk louder or longer. Thinking they have to really get people's approval with this one, they'll embellish a story or lie to keep the listener's attention. When they have been rejected over and over, they'll develop a compulsion for talking, and then it becomes addictive. If they can't find someone to talk to, they think they'll go crazy! They haven't learned to love themselves as God loves them, and are still plugged into those whose approval they seek.

Cholerics will work their hands to the bone to gain approval. Sometimes they are on a performance trip for their boss, sometimes for society in general, sometimes even "for God." Their strength as hard workers becomes a weakness as they let other things in their life slip away while they spend more and more hours at the office. This imbalance becomes compulsion, and eventually, addiction. *Cholerics* are society's "workaholics."

Rejected *Melancholies* will carry their need for perfection to an extreme, often becoming obsessed with their looks or abilities, unable to appreciate others who are not "perfect." They'll spend hours in front of the mirror or on a project, striving for perfection. This is their way of seeking acceptance and avoiding rejection.

Rejected *Phlegmatics* hide behind their peaceful natures. They procrastinate, becoming more and more passive and fearful of conflict. Obsessed with keeping peace at all costs, they withdraw from life and become mentally, emotionally and physically isolated. In isolation, no one can reject them.

WHO'S IN CONTROL?

Powerful Cholerics who are allowed to be in charge of everyone and everything in their lives get comfortable in that situation, and are lulled by a false sense of being "in control." The real reason they feel in control is because the people in their lives have chosen and are continuing to choose to let them lead. *Sometimes we choose to let others lead because it gives us a sense of security and keeps us from being rejected by them.* When a formerly passive husband begins to take a stand with an aggressive wife, or ex-wife, she usually becomes afraid. The anger she may display is really fear based, and is an effort to keep the control she thinks she's had and may be losing. Her efforts to control will usually intensify at that point. The breaking away is painful and scary to both people.

Choleric Women/Phlegmatic Men

A Choleric ex-wife who loses "control" in divorce, will usually double her efforts to regain that control, and will be angered every time control is, or is perceived to be, threatened. Since her ex-husband usually did what she said when they were married, and now he doesn't, she blames the new wife for her influence over the ex-husband. The "old queen" having wielded the power of the crown for so long, usually rallies her forces to overturn the new queen. Her "army" can include an ex-mother-in-law who's on her side, the kids who try to make Dad feel guilty or who reject their new stepmother, and of course the powerful divorce attorney.

A Choleric new wife, who observes her peaceful, passive husband give in to his ex-wife out of fear of conflict, fear of rejection, guilt, or feelings of failure, will also feel loss of control. When a husband surrenders to or prioritizes issues with the ex-wife, his new wife shares his feelings of powerlessness.

Phlegmatic Women/Choleric Men

All of the personalities have ways of being "in control." Cholerics control by threats of anger. Phlegmatics control by withdrawal or procrastination. Sanguines control by charm; Melancholies by threats of moodiness.

If the ex-wife is Phlegmatic, she may keep her sense of

being in control by telling you she'll cooperate (keeping the peace momentarily), but then procrastinating. A Phlegmatic ex-wife can also remain "in control" by feigning helplessness and having her ex-husband rush in to take care of the matter. Even though he divorced her and is married to someone else, she can still get him over to her house to hang up those Christmas lights!

WHY WE NEED TO UNDERSTAND THE PERSONALITIES

Problems in our marriages, and problems with the ex-spouse, can be largely alleviated by learning to understand the natural tendencies of the people we're dealing with. Obviously, the more we know and understand about our spouse, the better chance we have of succeeding at marriage. It's helpful to know why an ex-wife behaves the way she does so you can reach a greater understanding of her needs and motives. Other benefits of understanding the personalities are:

You Can Begin to Understand and Love Yourself

The "second greatest commandment" given to us is, "Love your neighbor as yourself." If we don't learn to love and accept ourselves on the same level God does, we'll never be able to really love or accept others. *The first step in loving yourself is knowing yourself!* Knowing our identity in Christ and understanding the personality He gave us helps us accept ourselves just as we are. I can learn to appreciate others' strengths, but enjoy the freedom to focus on my natural Sanguine gifts.

You Can Stop Rejecting Others and Start Loving Them

It used to bug me to see my husband observe a situation and take his time responding. "Do something!" I'd impatiently demand. Why couldn't he respond as quickly as I would? Well, talk about pride. After learning the personalities, I now know that many times when I jump into a quick response I overlook important details, or don't stop to consider the consequences.

That's when my fast-thinking, quick Choleric strength becomes a weakness. Then, when I am in a real emotional pickle, my slow thinking, patient husband, who carefully watched what was happening, steps in and helps me out of my jam. Now when I see him moving slower than I would, I stop to look at my own attitude and actions: maybe *I am moving too quickly*. I used to look down my nose at people who were, what I assumed to be, indecisive or passive. I now realize those traits, *if not carried to extremes*, are actually powerful strengths. I no longer reject my husband for who God made him to be: a Peaceful Phlegmatic.

You Can Quit Taking Rejection So Personally

Each of the four personalities has different emotional needs. When my husband has put in a long, stressful day, all he wants is the couch and some peace and quiet. After my day at work, I can still come home and iron our clothes, do his laundry and sew while I watch TV. I used to look at the list of things he'd promise to do for me, see him lying on the couch and think, "He doesn't love me enough to do what I asked of him." It wasn't about me, though.

As a Peaceful Phlegmatic, my huband's emotional needs were for rest and quiet in the evening. He'd reached his limit for the day. My husband loves me very much and would do anything I asked. He just isn't going to do them all right away. He doesn't always have the same emotional energy level I do. The Phlegmatic is "The Mule." When he's ready to sit down, NOBODY can make him budge! The Choleric is "The Bull." He keeps bashing his head against the wall and doesn't know when to stop. Both can be strengths, both can be weaknesses. Once I understood my husband's responses were based on his emotional needs, and not rejection of me personally, I stopped reading rejection into situations where there was none.

You Can Begin to Help Meet Others' Emotional Needs

After learning the personalities and their emotional needs, Tom and I were able to show love to each other in new ways,

The Royal Treatment

by being aware of what the other really needed, not what we *thought* they needed.

Learning to communicate to the other person's personality is much more effective than communicating yours. Loud, dominating Cholerics can tone their voices down when dealing with Phlegmatics. Always-joking Sanguines can get a little more serious with Melancholies. Next time you talk to the ex-wife, try meeting her on her level of communication, not yours.

If you know the ex-wife is Choleric and needs to be appreciated for all her hard work, or needs to feel in charge, you can find something that she's worked hard at and show appreciation, in a note or on the phone. If you're changing her visitation schedule to fit in your summer vacation, offer her two or three options so she can feel she has some control in her choice of dates or times. Be careful not to fall into the trap of giving her insincere compliments just to "keep her happy." Be genuine or be quiet.

If the ex-wife is Phlegmatic, don't push her for an immediate response to your requests. She may need extra time to process things. Even though you'd like a quick answer, try to meet her emotional needs. Don't forget to give some reasonable deadline, though, to avoid prolonged procrastination.

Chapter 19

How Husbands and Wives Damage Each Other's Spirits

The "Royal Treatment" in a marriage begins with the husband and wife's attitude toward each other, for attitudes give birth to action. When you ask a husband or wife what they want from their spouse, they may not always have a ready answer, but will usually know right away what they don't want! Therefore, learning HOW to treat spouses like kings and queens, means addressing what NOT to do.

THE TEN WAYS A HUSBAND DAMAGES HIS WIFE'S SPIRIT

He does not give her first priority in his life.

When a wife feels she has to compete with her husband's job, ex-wife, mother, friends, hobbies or children, she will be hurt. Most men have their priorities out of order because no one ever taught them the proper order. *Men: Make your wife your first earthly priority!*

The Royal Treatment

He withholds praise or forgets to praise her attempts to please him.

Wives feel unnecessary and used when they are not recognized for their efforts to please their husbands. *Men: Begin to notice her efforts in the little things, and praise her!*

He doesn't provide spiritual leadership.

Reading the Bible, praying and attending church are good actions. However, a true spiritual leader will develop an attitude of Christlike compassion, tenderness and sensitivity to all his wife's needs. *Men: True spiritual leadership involves meeting her physical, financial and emotional needs as well!*

He doesn't provide material security for the wife and children.

It's become more common to see men who aren't willing to provide for their families. A wife who works outside the home has a lot of stress on her. It's not a sin for her to work, but it may not be God's best for her. When a wife is depended on to provide income for the daily needs of her family, other areas suffer. The quality of housekeeping, meals, attention to the children and the sexual relationship with her husband are the first areas to deteriorate. Whether it's the husband making more money, or the whole family living on a lower budget, there may be ways to allow the wife to stay home. *Men: Challenge yourselves to establish a new lifestyle where your wife is free to stay at home with the children.*

He refuses to seek her counsel before making serious decisions.

When a husband leaves his wife out of major personal or family decisions, his message to her is one of rejection. She feels unnecessary and disrespected. A wise man frequently seeks his wife's counsel. *Men: Start asking your wife's opinion; she may be able to give you a new perspective!*

How Husbands and Wives Damage Each Other's Spirits

He doesn't assume responsibility in disciplining the children.

The wife becomes resentful toward a man who does not help her teach or discipline the children. If he takes the kids' side, the wife will feel he is being disloyal and putting the emotional demands of the children ahead of her, as well as trying to win them to himself. Some fathers will back the wife up when she's around, but when he's alone with the children, he will bend or relax the rules. This lack of consistency also damages the children, which makes the wife even more resentful. *Men: Always back your wife up in front of the children and don't set her up to be the "bad guy."*

He is unfair or overly strict with the children.

When the husband's discipline is too harsh, the wife will by her nature try to defend the child. This creates a wounded spirit in both the mother and the child. *Men: Be firm in your disciplinary actions, but gentle in your attitude.*

He is not considerate of her busy schedule.

Sometimes the husband is insensitive to his wife's need to have time alone. Most wives have a full work schedule just keeping up with the meals, shopping, laundry and child care. When the husband makes plans for what he wants to do without considering his wife's schedule, she feels he is selfish and uncaring of her needs. *Men: Take inventory of your wife's schedule before you make plans.*

He lacks inner discipline.

A wife loses respect and admiration for her husband when she senses in him a lack of discipline resulting in anger or moral weakness. Continual financial mishandling or career crises compound the situation. *Men: Push yourselves toward continued mental and emotional growth for yourself and your family.*

The Royal Treatment

He has a critical spirit toward his wife.

The husband should not criticize his wife in private or in public. Her weakness can be discussed in such a manner that her character is not attacked. *Men: If you need to discuss your wife's weaknesses, do it in a loving and noncritical manner, and only with her.*

SEVEN WAYS A WIFE DAMAGES HER HUSBAND'S SPIRIT

She doesn't forgive him for past failures.

The husband always knows when his wife hasn't really forgiven him for his past mistakes. Often the wife will send the message, "You should have listened to me in the first place," or, "We wouldn't be in this mess if it wasn't for you." *Women: Understand that men will fail, but they can learn and grow from failure.*

She demonstrates a continual anxiety over his decisions.

When the wife is uptight about her husband's decisions, she displays a lack of trust in the Lord. When she verbally questions and disapproves of his decisions in a critical manner, she becomes his conscience, and every husband fights his conscience. This will cause the husband to become defensive and react negatively to his wife. *Women: Lovingly counsel your husband, but be willing to let him lead.*

She is insensitive to his concerns.

When a wife does not show loving care toward his concerns, he feels used and unimportant. When he spends most of his time trying to support the family, his wife would be wise to show interest in his career. Many women get too caught up in the stresses of their own daily worries to think about their husband's problems. *Women: Stop and ask your husband what he's worried about. Don't counsel, just listen.*

How Husbands and Wives Damage Each Other's Spirits

She's not a good stewardess of the resources he provides.

When a wife doesn't take good care of the home and other material things her husband supplies, or spends excessively, he senses a spirit of ingratitude. This causes him to lose interest in providing for his family's needs. The wife that refuses to cook healthy meals, keep a clean home and take care of her appearance is telling her husband, "I don't respect you." *Women: Develop an atitude of gratitude and show it in how you manage yourself and the family.*

She doesn't show appreciation for the little things.

When a wife expects "extras" from her husband, his motivation to give them decreases. She may be angry at him for something else and will "punish" him by refusing to acknowledge his attempts to please her. When he tries to romance you with little gifts, gestures or special time, take time to focus on what he's doing and show appreciation. If you are distracted or angry, take time to clear the air. *Women: No matter where you are emotionally, genuinely thank him for his efforts.*

She fosters a spirit of disloyalty to him in the children.

When a wife is angry at her husband, and feels the need to vent her frustrations, she may be tempted to criticize him to the children. This attempt to gather the forces on "her side" damages the respect children have for their father. When the children lose respect for him, this destroys their loving response to him. *Women: Honor and protect your husband's relationship with his children. When you're angry with him, keep the children out of it.* Both parents should back each other up in front of the children. Wives, if you don't agree with your husband's disciplinary efforts, talk to him afterwards in private. Don't argue or defend the children. Don't go to them after he's left the room and make excuses, criticize him or bargain with the kids.

The Royal Treatment

She expects him to satisfy all her needs and remember everything.

Some wives are not sensitive to all the pressures of being head of a family. Some have been taught to expect their husbands to be "fantasy" husbands, never forgetting birthdays and never making mistakes. Most husbands want to remember all the little details, but can't do a perfect job because they are human! *Women: Cut him some slack. If there's something you can do for yourself, do it. Better yet, do something for him at the same time!*

Chapter 20

How a Husband Provides
for His Wife

✠

he three steps a husband must take to love his
wife the way God intended are:

Provide for her
Protect her
Present her

Most husbands would be more than willing to follow these
steps, but have never been told what they are or how to imple-
ment them. Not only have women remained a "mystery" to
men, how to love them can be just as mysterious. The next
chapters help take the guesswork out of the simple biblical
command, "Love your wife."

THE LOVE QUESTIONS

One of my favorite parts of counseling at New Life Dynamics
Christian Counseling Center in Phoenix, Arizona, was "The
Love Questions." After Tom and I learned to break free of our
bitterness to people and past circumstances, we reached deeper levels of love and intimacy. We began to establish weekly
and monthly rituals which would help us stay "in love" with

The Royal Treatment

each other even through the normal ups and downs of married life. The counseling program teaches husbands to meet their wives' needs on five levels: *mental, emotional, sexual, material and spiritual.*

At first weekly, and now once a month or so, Tom tells me he'd like to set aside some time for the "Love Questions." We sit in a quiet spot, turn off the TV and put the phone recorder on. Tom has a tablet and pen ready for writing. He takes my hand, gives it a little squeeze and looks me right in the eye. "Honey," he begins . . . and then he asks me the five love questions:

Love Question No. 1
"What Can I Do to Free Your Mind from Worry and Anxiety?"

It might take practice at first to get in touch with the things that might be bothering a wife, but most women have no problems expressing their worries or anxieties. A helpful mental checklist is "work, family, kids, school, friendships, house," or something to that effect. Wives need to remember not just to vent their emotions, but to suggest some specific action the husband can take to meet her needs.

Love Question No. 2
"What Can I Do to Free You from Feelings of Inferiority or Inadequacy?"

This is usually the "hot spot" where the ex-wife (or even mother-in-law) comes into the picture. Typical answers for new wives include:

"When you talk about the good times you used to have with her, it makes me feel jealous. Please don't discuss those in front of me."

"When you help the kids buy her a birthday present, but don't have them pick one for me, I feel rejected by them and you. Please teach the kids to honor me, too."

"When you take her side in front of me, I feel rejected and angry. Please back me up no matter what."

"At school functions you always forget to introduce me to the teachers. Please introduce me as the kids' stepmother."

Love Question No. 3
"What Can I Start to Do, or Stop Doing, to Please You Sexually?"

This is an area where many women need to exercise boldness in expressing their needs. There is no room for false purity or piety.

"Honey, when you grab me like that, I'm offended. I need a tender touch."

"Well, when you don't talk to me all day and then expect me to warm up to you, I get angry. Could you start some love talk earlier in the evening?"

"I can't respond when I'm angry. Can we talk things out first?"

"I like it a little harder/slower/faster." "I'd like to take a bath with you." "I like music on." "I don't like that music."

These are all specific requests that will help a husband meet his wife's needs.

Love Question No. 4
"What Can I Do to Meet Your Needs Materially?"

I usually go to town on this one. I know I won't always get what I'd like, but I figure my husband should know what would please me! Just be careful not to be ungrateful for what you receive or to burden him with guilt by requesting things above your means.

"A housekeeper once a month, if possible."

"A $25 increase in my monthly clothes shopping budget."

"I'd like to start getting my nails/hair done."

"I'd like a massage once a month. Can we afford that?"

The Royal Treatment

Love Question No. 5
"What Can I Do to Start Leading You Spiritually?"

The first answer I learned to tell my husband was, "begin to meet my *other* needs." I don't want a husband who will pompously read from the Bible at the dinner table, but refuse to let me have some help with the housework if I know we can afford it. I don't care if he takes us all to church on Sunday if he won't stick up for me in front of his ex-wife. The Bible commands men to "Love your wives," not NEGLECT them.

One of the most frequent responses I give to this last love question is for the children, not myself. I don't want to be the only one teaching my children about God. Unfortunately, many men leave the training of the children in *all* areas up to the women. There are just some things that can be taught best by, and sometimes only by, the father of the family. After all, every child's relationship with his Heavenly Father will at first be patterned after his relationship with his earthly father.

WHAT HAPPENS WHEN THE HUSBAND RESPONDS TO THE LOVE QUESTIONS

God gives not only authority to the husband, but the full responsibility of loving and caring for his wife. As she sees her husband express his love in words as well as action, she will automatically respond to him with love, honor and respect. She will begin to feel secure and satisfied in her marriage.

God created women to desire their husband's leadership and protection. It doesn't matter if a woman is a Choleric personality (assertive, natural leader) or Phlegmatic (passive, natural follower); both desire strong, loving leadership in a husband.

"Your desire will be for your husband, and he will rule over you."
Genesis 3:16b

Chapter 21

How a Husband Protects His Wife

❖

P rotection isn't just an alarm system or a dead bolt on the front door. When a husband loves his wife, he will protect her mentally, physically, emotionally, sexually, financially and spiritually.

MENTAL AND PHYSICAL PROTECTION

The obvious protection a man provides is never being verbally or physically abusive to his wife. However, there are many more areas where a man can and should provide physical protection for his wife.

Husbands should make sure her car works safely and gets regular tune-ups. The house should be secure, and the health insurance should be paid up. If she is sick, he should insist she see a doctor. If she has a problem with overeating, alcohol, drug or other addiction, he will help her get into a recovery program. If she refuses to go, he will get himself into a support program for spouses and families.

If he smokes and she doesn't, he will keep his smoke outside and out of the family cars. If they live in an unsafe neigh-

The Royal Treatment

borhood, he will do everything he can to move the family to a better area. If he is away for periods of time, he will have someone check in on them, or have a male friend or relative available to help in an emergency.

If the ex-wife is abusive to his new wife or children, he will minimize contact between them, or seek legal action to protect them. If she harasses his new wife, he will risk his ex-wife's anger or legal threats to protect his new wife and/or family.

EMOTIONAL PROTECTION

When she is being verbally abused, he defends her. If she is emotionally worn down, he makes sure she gets the rest she needs. When they are at a party and someone makes a derogatory comment to or about her, he will defend her, ask for an apology or otherwise support her.

When the stepchildren report their mother's negative criticism of her, he will defend her to the children. He will also teach the children to have a grateful and loving spirit toward their stepmother.

When they are in a family situation and the ex-wife is present, he will be sensitive to his wife's emotional needs. He will not leave her alone or unattended for long periods at parties or other social gatherings, nor exclude her from conversations.

If a man's wife ever comes up in conversation where her character is being attacked, his response should be, *"My wife is not up for discussion!"*

SEXUAL PROTECTION

A husband will never cause physical harm to his wife in any way. He will protect her from perversity and shield her from harassment by others. A loving husband will not force his wife to perform acts which are unnatural or uncomfortable for her, nor will he insist on her using pornographic materials or aids in their lovemaking. A husband also shows love to his wife by keeping himself clean and disease free.

How a Husband Protects His Wife

FINANCIAL PROTECTION

Loving husbands will keep the family on a budget, protecting them from financial disaster. He will make sure the family "needs" are paid for before the family "wants." He will avoid excessive use of credit and keep what credit they do have in good standing.

Husbands who love their wives will make sure she has sufficient grocery and spending money for herself. When there is "extra" money to spend, he will consider her special requests with his own. He will not place the ex-wife's or children's financial "wants" before hers. He will make every attempt to provide some type of life insurance or other protection for his wife in the event of his untimely death. He will start a retirement savings program so that she is not left bereft in her later years.

If a husband is ordered through the divorce agreement to carry separate life insurance policies on himself for his children from the previous marriage, the ex-wife does not have to be named as trustee. Any third party can be named. This will help ensure that the money will be properly administered for the children in the event of his death. Usually such policies are ordered by the court agreement at specific amounts. Over time the benefits may grow to exceed the original policy coverage amount. If so, the "excess" can be assigned to the new wife or third party. Check with your insurance agent.

SPIRITUAL PROTECTION

To protect his wife, a husband should pray for her every day. He should pray for all her needs. He should pray for the grace to love her more each day, to be patient, tolerant and nonjudgmental. A husband should pray to know his wife better each day and to discern what is best for her and the family. He should pray for the grace to help him be the man, husband and father God intended.

Recommended Reading: Margorie Engel & Diana Gould, *The Divorce Decisions Workbook* (New York: McGraw Hill, 1992).

Chapter 22

How a Husband Presents His Wife

✣

"**L**ONG LIVE THE QUEEN"

The trumpets blared joyfully throughout the kingdom. Throngs of citizens waved their gaily colored flags and cried out in anticipation of the royal celebration. Inside the palace, the great hall was lined with lords and ladies dressed in sumptuous suits and gowns, their heads adorned with feathers and powdered wigs, their necks with precious jewels. The murmur grew to a loud buzz as they awaited the first glimpse of their new queen.

Suddenly the king and his queen appeared, and a hush fell over the crowd. With necks craned and mouths agape, everyone oohed and ahhed. She was the most beautiful creature they had ever seen. The king stood proud and tall, his mighty chest emblazoned with medals, his powerful arm held out firm and strong to hold the arm of the queen. With fierce pride, the king took slow, deliberate steps through the midst of the parted crowd, toward the pair of golden thrones. The new queen glided gracefully at her husband's side as she smiled at her royal subjects. He led her up the steps as the chamberlains arranged her train around the throne. She sat as the king took his place at her side, still standing. Presenting her to his subjects, the king called joyfully to the people, "Long live the queen!" In unison they joined him in his praise. "LONG LIVE THE QUEEN!"

HOW TO PRESENT A WIFE

Fairytale or not, every woman experiences the feeling of being the most beautiful creature in the kingdom when her husband proudly presents her to the world. When a man honors his wife's virtues, considers her value as "far above rubies" and takes pride in the fact that she is his wife, she will naturally respond in love and devotion to her "king."

In remarriage, the husband needs to "present" his wife to the members of his family, his friends and community. Here are some practical ways to make a new wife feel like a queen.

PRESENT HER TO THE EX-WIFE

The first time the ex-wife and new wife meet may be uncomfortable for one, both or all three parties. The husband should be as sensitive to his wife, and his ex-wife, in their introduction as possible. Even if they have seen each other at a distance, a new wife will feel honored when her husband introduces her, by name, to his ex-wife when he has the chance.

If the husband avoids this, the new wife may feel he is embarrassed, ashamed or guilty. It's helpful to plan ahead and be prepared to ignore any negative response by the ex-wife, remembering instead her own insecurity or pain.

The husband should never gloat or otherwise attempt to humiliate or anger his ex-wife either in public or private. While he can't be responsible for his ex-wife's feelings, he can and should be sensitive to them.

PRESENT HER TO THE CHILDREN

The husband should introduce their stepmother to them without the ex-wife present if there is still bitterness or conflict.

How a Husband Presents His Wife

One fun way to help the children get to know his wife would be to share the story of how he met her and why he loves her so much, and some of the fun or silly things they did when they were courting. With younger children this can be a warm, loving time of bonding. For older children it can bring out their anger, fear, insecurities and even jealousy of their new parent. Husbands and wives should allow the older children to vent their feelings in a constructive way and shouldn't try to force "instant intimacy." Husbands should not, however, back down from their love and respect for their new wives, nor minimize his new wife as first priority to the children.

Try to avoid the phrase "your *real* mom" or "your *real* dad." Although it's the most commonly used, it reinforces both in the speaker and the listener that one parent is real and the other is "fake," "not real," "false," or an "imposter." Some husbands, when talking about both mothers to their children will use the women's first names. Some say "your mom" and "your stepmom." Try to help the kids avoid using the word "real." They, too, can learn to say Mom and Stepmom.

Let the children see you hug and kiss your new wife. Let them see all the normal, loving interchanges between a man and wife that are appropriate for their ages.

When you take a family trip, never let any of the children or your mother sit in the front seat. The front passenger seat is for your wife. When you go out with another couple, don't make the two women sit in back. Although some women may automatically take the back seats, ask your wife if she would like to sit up front with you, and tell her you would prefer it. It's a small gesture, but sends a powerful message.

Don't let the kids have the best seat in front of the TV. Ask your wife what her favorite chair is, and announce in front of the whole family that whenever your wife wants to sit down, that place is hers alone. If they are old enough, you may have the children do the dishes for her after dinner. Let the children see you honor her and they will be more likely to follow suit. When the children see two married people honoring and putting each other first all the time, they will be

The Royal Treatment

learning how to love their own future husbands or wives the way God intended.

THE FAMILY

Whenever there is a divorce, family members often feel compelled to "take sides." The new wife may be met with anything ranging from a cool reception to an outright snubbing. When this happens, the husband should make every effort not to place his new wife in a situation where this could occur again. If they have dinner with his parents, and there is tension or conversation meant to embarrass her, the husband needs to respond immediately in her defense. Not in anger, but setting firm boundaries.

"Mother, Marsha is my new wife and deserves your courtesy. Your bringing up my ex-wife is not appropriate, and I would like you to stop it."

If Mom gets angry, hostile or defensive, the husband should try putting his arm around her and looking her right in the eye. "Mom, the past is past. I understand you're having trouble with this, but I love Marsha. Won't you try to, too?"

If she still refuses, the husband should get up and take his wife home. He should tell his parents firmly but lovingly, "Mom, Dad, I want to visit you, but it seems like you need some time to accept Marsha. Please call me when you are ready to have us over again."

Give them some time and a second chance. It may take awhile, but most family members will begin to open the door after they process their own anger, guilt and grief. Some family or friends will never welcome the new spouse. In that case, the husband and his new wife must complete the grieving process over the loss of their relationship with those people and move on.

THE COMMUNITY

Husbands, take your new wife to school and introduce her to the children's teachers and coaches. Make sure you both get on the mailing lists for special announcements, school pictures and other parent invitations. Take her to parent/teacher conferences, school plays and sports activities. Sit next to her, not the ex-wife. If there is still bitterness from the ex-wife or insecurity in the new wife, don't put yourself physically between the two in a seating arrangement at a public event. Choose another place or trade seats.

Put the new wife's name on the list of people authorized to pick the children up from school or daycare facilities. If she needs a picture ID, make sure she has no trouble getting authorized. Tell the school to call her in case of emergency when you can't be reached. Give the school your home phone number and your new wife's work phone. It's good for the child to have mother, father and stepparents on these lists, because in case of a real emergency, any available loving parent is better than none!

Introduce her to other significant people in the community as well, including the children's doctor and dentist, their friends and their friends' parents.

❧

Chapter 28

How a Wife Honors Her Husband

⊱✠⊰

onor your husband, love and obey;
Give him to God and get out of God's
way! "

When a man provides for, protects and presents his wife, the wife will find it easy to respond to him in the way God calls her. The wife's repsonses to her husband are the same as her responses to God:

Reverence

Dependence

Obedience

REVERENCE IS THE WIFE'S FIRST RESPONSE

When a husband begins to meet his wife's needs in every area of her life, she will naturally develop a grateful spirit and begin to *reverence* him as her husband. This is followed by a healthy *dependence* (interdependence) on him.

The last response is often the hardest for many women, especially if they are by nature the more assertive personality, have been abused in past relationships, or have never developed

The Royal Treatment

a "meek and quiet spirit." For wives, *obedience* to a husband is the same as obedience to God. Reluctance to obey is usually rooted in fear and lack of faith. Women are called, however, to obey (what they know they should do) even when they don't trust their feelings.

Reverencing a Husband Begins with an Attitude of Honor

The wife's three basic responses (actions) are each based upon a specific attitude. To be able to "reverence" her husband, the wife's attitude must be: *"I view my husband as the tool God will use to build into my life character qualities I lack."* Viewing her husband as a tool, not a weapon, will help her appreciate what God is doing in her through her husband.

The Tortoise and the Hare-Dryer

Tom's slow and careful approach to life used to irritate me! I wished he could move a little faster, make his mind up sooner and pick up his pace! I took a little too much pride in the fact I was sharp, quick and able to accomplish twice as much as the average person in a day. Why couldn't my husband be more like *me*?

Although I'd learned that Tom's slower Phlegmatic approach to life had its own unique strengths, in practice I still had an attitude of Choleric superiority. I hadn't really learned to *reverence* my husband in many areas. My attitude changed on a trip to San Diego.

"Let's GO!" I excitedly urged my husband and the kids. My stepson and one of his cousins were going with us on a weekend vacation and we had tickets to the theater that night. I'd loaded up the car with my overnight bag, the kids' suitcases and was waiting impatiently for my husband who was still in the house, locking up. When Tom got into the car, he began his usual ritual of asking if we'd forgotten anything. I would always feel quite insulted by what I interpreted as his insinuation that I was less than efficient.

How a Wife Honors Her Husband

"Yes, yes, yes," I replied hastily when he asked if I had the theater tickets, the sunscreen and the boys' dress clothes. "What about your hairdryer?" he asked one last time.

I froze. My hairdryer! I'd forgotten to pack it! I'd be in such a panic at the hotel that night before the theater if I came out of the shower and had no hairdryer! It would be too late to go buy one. Tom knew that about me. Once at a hotel I'd nearly gone into a frenzy when I couldn't find my hairdryer, although I found it minutes later. Tom had remembered my response, and was being careful to make sure everything would go smoothly for me on our weekend.

I raced into the house and got my hairdryer. The kids laughed as I got back into the car, leaned over into the driver's seat and began smothering Tom with kisses. "Oh, honey, thank you, thank you, *thank you!*" From that day on I began to honor Tom's careful and deliberate inventory taking, not just on our trips, but in every part of our life.

God was using Tom to teach me that my own hurried pace was nothing to be proud of. I learned some humility and a much deeper appreciation for taking life a little more slowly. The hairdryer incident has been only one of many ways God has used my husband to teach me some balance!

WHEN HUSBANDS ARE HARD TO HONOR

Kathy's husband, Wayne, was still uncomfortable about his new wife and his ex-wife being in the same room together. His ex-wife resented Kathy, and had never shown her any kindness. As a result, he often told Kathy to wait in the car when they dropped the kids off at their mothers, and he would go inside and chat for awhile, just to keep his ex-wife happy.

Kathy explained to her husband how sitting alone outside in the car made her feel, and that it was certainly not honoring her in front of the kids or his ex-wife. He acknowledged her feelings, but was still in too much emotional bondage to put his new wife's emotional needs before his. "Babe, please just trust me on this. It just makes things easier all the way around, okay?"

The Royal Treatment

Kathy felt rejected and emotionally abandoned, but had resolved to honor her husband. Still she teased him, "Next time I'm just going to walk in anyway!" Wayne just gave her a look. Kathy sat thoughtfully all the way home and searched for the character quality God might be trying to build in her. A "meek and quiet" spirit and patience immediately came to her mind. "Okay, God," she thought, "I will still let my husband know where I stand on this, but I will honor and obey his requests. Meanwhile, could you work on his heart?"

Over a year passed before Wayne finally realized how futile keeping his ex-wife happy was. Through counseling, Wayne had begun to realize the importance of honoring his new wife. Kathy's patience paid off. One night when taking the children back to their mother's, Wayne walked her up to the door with the kids. His ex-wife was not happy to see Kathy standing there, and only opened the screen door far enough for the kids to squeeze through. She said, "Bye," quickly and shut the door in their faces.

Kathy and Wayne had expected her response and did not react. Instead, Wayne started the car up, and before driving off, leaned over and kissed his wife, saying, "Thanks, Babe, for being patient with me all this time and not nagging me. I'm sorry it took me so long to see how foolish I've been. You're the best!"

Sometimes it's difficult to reverence a husband who is not following God's will for his life. But when a wife finds herself focusing on her husband's actions, it's time to focus on her own attitude. *She should ask herself what character quality God may be trying to build in her through her husband even when it is hard to honor him.*

Chapter 24

How a Wife Depends on Her Husband

n Stephen Covey's best-selling book, *The Seven Habits of Highly Effective People* (New York: Simon & Schuster, 1989), he defines the three levels of dependence.

Dependence — We begin life dependent on others to meet our basic needs. At this level of maturity, our focus is on others. We hold others responsible for meeting our needs.

Independence — As we mature, we begin to assume responsibility for meeting our own mental, emotional and physical needs.

Interdependence — The highest of the three levels, this phase reflects our willingness to assume full responsibility for our own needs, but also to work with others who may have a strength we don't, realizing that together we are more effective than apart.

DEPENDENCE IS THE WIFE'S SECOND RESPONSE

Dependence: The Attitude

> *"I prayerfully position myself under my husband's authority as God's ordained leader."*

The Royal Treatment

In accepting the husband as leader of the marriage and family, it is "interdependence" that is the goal. This is the biblical principle of mutual submission in action. Ephesians 5 addresses this. "Wives, submit to your husbands as to the Lord. For the husband is the head of the wife as Christ is the head of the church . . . ." (vv. 22,23) And then, "Husbands, love your wives, just as Christ loved the church and gave himself up for her . . . . husbands ought to love their wives as their own bodies" (vv. 25, 28). The act of loving on the husband's part facilitates and encourages the wife's submission to him.

This mutual interdependence is healthy, not harmful. Husbands do not smother their wives, and wives do not unrealistically expect husbands to meet all of their needs singlehandedly. Only Christ can meet all of our needs.

MONEY DEMONS

Money issues are usually among the first where husbands and wives disagree, and where women are tempted to try to control the outcome if they don't feel they can depend on their husbands.

In her book, *Money Demons* (New York: Bantam/Doubleday, 1994), Dr. Susan Forward (author of *Men Who Hate Women and the Women Who Love Them*), cautions women not to rescue money-reckless men, as the "emotional boundaries between the two of you will blur as surely as the financial ones." She continues, "When you love a man, you can't help but empathize with him. When he hurts, you hurt. When he suffers, you suffer. It is only natural for you to want to help solve his problems — not only for his peace of mind, but for your own."

The problem with a wife trying to control her husband's leadership, is that she is assuming responsibility for his problems — problems that God may intend to promote emotional growth in the husband.

When the wife interferes with her husband's natural learning process, she is not only getting in God's way, she's actually preventing her husband from becoming the man she would like him to be.

How a Wife Depends on Her Husband

WHAT WIVES SHOULD DO

Every wife has an opinion of what her husband should or shouldn't do. Every wife has the right to express her opinion fully and to be heard by her husband. No wife has the right to manipulate, nag, remind, threaten, guilt, shame or otherwise try to control what actions her husband takes.

Tell your husband how important it is to you and the family that he maintain good credit, but allow him to fail. Some people don't learn as quickly as others. Remember *repetition can be the greatest torture or the greatest teacher.*

Don't become his conscience or his mother. A man fights his conscience and must leave his mother.

Let him be late with the child support and have his ex-wife threaten court action. Let him fail to bring the children home on time to their mother's and face possible arrest.

Remember, with rights come responsibilities. It is a wife's responsibility to allow her husband his right to make and learn from his own mistakes. This is where patience is cultivated.

DEPENDENCE: BEING WILLING TO LOSE IN ORDER TO WIN

Let's put the shoe on the other foot. Suppose you wanted to start a gift basket business in your home with a girlfriend. After relaying all the information to your husband, and after careful consideration he advised you he thought the business idea was fine, but that he didn't think your girlfriend was a good potential business partner. He thought you would end up doing all the work and that she would not follow through on her commitments.

After listening to his discouraging advice, would you want him to order you not to go into business? Or would you appreciate a response such as:

"Honey, I don't think it's a good idea, and you just heard the reasons why. I'm willing though, to stand behind your venture no matter what happens. If what I think will happen does happen, I won't hold it up to you, but would hope you'd be open to learning from it. Okay?"

The Royal Treatment

Of course you would. That's all I'm saying you should do for your husband. Give each other room to make mistakes. Stand by each other. Never say, "I told you so!"

Chapter 25

A Wife's Most Powerful Tool: Obedience

The Attitude: *"In following the leadership of my husband I follow God's leadership through him."*

THE CHORE CHART

My husband and I both work full-time jobs. We both pitch in with the household chores, but sometimes I felt that I was getting stuck with the heavier load. Take the dishes. I like to pop things in the microwave, heat 'em and eat 'em. Tom likes to prepare a thorough six-course meal that invariably includes something fried. Guess who makes the bigger mess, dirties more pots and pans, and covers the counter with a thin film of cholesterol?

Well, I'd agreed to doing the dishes as part of the chore split, but was regretting the fact that after a long day at work I had to clean up all his pots and pans. He didn't have as much to clean up after I cooked, and I thought this was quite unfair! Part of the reason I was becoming disgruntled was that I was also doing all his laundry. He works outside and changes clothes twice a day. I kept comparing my little pile of leotards and socks to his huge mountain of towels, jeans and T-shirts that you have to fold-right-out-of-the-dryer-or-they'll-wrinkle!

After we went through the counseling at New Life Dynamics, Tom spent a week doing all the chores he'd either expected me or asked me to do. I did *nothing*. He cooked, cleaned, shopped and ironed. This taught him the full extent of everything I did, and gave him a clear understanding of what was necessary to run the house.

After the week, Tom made a list of all the chores and decided which he would do and which would be mine. First, though, I told him the ones I wanted and why, and then ended my requests with, "I trust you will be fair, honest and not hurt me in any way." Then I agreed to cheerfully accept his leadership. There was no power struggle. There was no insisting or resisting. It was all in Tom's hands.

He took over the bookkeeping, told me he'd appreciate me not committing our time to dinner at the folk's house without checking with him and asked me to continue doing the laundry. He took the dishes, the yard, and of course, the trash!

I was thrilled at being relieved of both the bill paying and the dishes. As a result of his fairness and consideration of my feelings, he gets the best laundry job a man could get, and I'm happy never to make plans for us without checking with him first! *We learned to honor each other through my submission to God and him.*

The "Me Generation"

So many of today's wedding ceremonies drop the traditional "love, honor and obey" from the recitation of vows. The Women's Liberation movement which began in the 1960s, challenged women to get out from under their husband's thumbs, and asserted there's no need to obey any man!

Active Obedience vs. Passive Obedience

God never intended women to obey by accepting abuse. God intended women to obey their husband's choices and decisions regarding the care of the family, allowing him to make and learn from his own mistakes. Still, for many women, obedience is little more palatable than the dreaded and woefully misunderstood, "submission." But obedience is what God requests from ALL his creatures. There are spiritual laws, natural laws and man-made laws that require our obedience. If we don't obey the speed limit, we'll get a ticket or have a wreck. If we don't obey the laws of nature, we may drown or burn ourselves.

Passive Obedience

Obedience on the level God talks about is not a mindless, empty-headed, passive servitude.

Active Obedience

Obedience on God's level is an active, living, loving TRUST.

WHEN THE HUSBAND FAILS

I will not violate my conscience for Tom, but I will submit myself to him in any other way he requests, of course after he listens to my counsel!

I agree to let Tom bounce a check, not pay a bill on time or forget to register the car. I won't refuse to accept his decision about how we spend our money or where we'll go on vacation. If, however, I think Tom is taking advantage of me, or carrying his authority a little too far, I use the "Love Question" time to calmly explain my feelings. Because he has also committed to loving me and making every effort to meet my needs, I know we will both be working toward a balanced and healthy relationship.

When husbands abuse their wives, lie about money and repeatedly make foolish family decisions, women are *not* instructed by God to lie down and accept this behavior. God gave us a head, a heart and insight that men sometimes don't have, and he expects us to use them!

The Royal Treatment

Wise wives should learn how to set boundaries with their husbands such as:

"I won't stay in the house when you scream like that. I will take the car and return in an hour."

When she comes back, she should insist on counseling.

"I believe we both need some counseling. Our marriage is the most important thing to me, and I will do whatever needs doing to get us back on track. Will you please see how much we can scrape out of the budget to cover a few months' sessions?"

If he refuses counseling, the wife should go by herself to learn how to protect herself and the children if things get worse.

If he is verbally, emotionally, financially, physically or sexually abusing you or the children, don't let anyone tell you to "go back and submit to him as the Bible says." Healthy submission has boundaries. Passive submission is self-abuse. It's a total disregard of ourselves and our children as God's precious creatures.

Chapter 26

The Royal Promises

✦

Our wedding vows pale in comparison to the *new promises* Tom and I have made to each other through the counseling process. Through the new promises we have established a new relationship, and our "old" marriage, one that first struggled with bitterness, fears, and guilt, is dead.

Tom agrees that God, faithful to his promises, has used our struggles to work good in our lives. Tom had experienced the same hopelessness that many men and women feel when they fail in their marriages, wondering if they will ever be able to have a happy marriage. We both learned that the Lord has made many wonderful promises to us, if only we take the time to avail ourselves of His gifts. Because God has made these covenants with His children as a sign of His love, we, too, make covenants with each other.

THE HUSBAND AND WIFE COVENANTS

When husbands and their new wives are ready to make the lifelong commitment to building and protecting the new marriage, I recommend a special ceremony in a quiet place, by

The Royal Treatment

the sea or over candlelight at a favorite restaurant. The husband's and wife's promises should be read out loud with direct eye contact and some tender touching.

Husband's First Commitment

"(Wife's Name), from this time on, I will not make any decisions that directly affect you or the children without first seeking your counsel. I will esteem your counsel as vital to our marriage."

Wife's First Commitment

"(Husband's Name), from this time on, I will not make any decisions that directly affect you or the children without first seeking your counsel. I will regard your counsel in light of God's loving leadership."

Wife's Response When Husband Seeks Her Counsel

"(Husband's Name), I have given you my opinion and I will stand beside you regardless of the decision you make. I'm trusting God not to allow you to hurt me or the children with your decision."

Wife's Second Commitment

"(Husband's Name), from this time on, I yield all rights to leadership in our home to you. I will only assume those that God gives me through you, my husband."

Husband's Second Commitment

"(Wife's Name), I gladly take responsibility for our family. By God's grace, I will love you as Christ loves the church."

This is the way a successful second marriage begins — a new commitment, a burial of past hurts, a new beginning.

The Royal Promises

❤ ❤ ❤

Remember Tim and Jane from the beginning of the book? Well, ten years later, they were reminiscing over a much different candlelight dinner. After applying the principles *of How to Be First in a Second Marriage*, they had both grown. This was indeed a night to remember . . . and they lived happily ever after!

About the Author

Rose Sweet has been an ex-wife, new wife and stepmom and knows firsthand the unique problems today's blended families face.

"When I found I came second to my husband's ex-wife I knew I needed a book that covered more than just step-parenting," Rose recalls. "Although the court papers had been signed years ago, my husband was still not emotionally divorced from his ex-spouse. We definitely needed help!"

Not finding help in her local bookstore, Rose decided to write the book herself. "I know there are millions of us out there who feel we are second in our marriages. We are angry, hurt, confused. This book can help anyone who wants to be first in their marriage."

With a particular heart for stepmoms and noncustodial parents, Rose has contributed articles to Focus on the Family's *Single Parent Magazine* and chapters to several book projects. In her *New Queen* Seminars, Rose helps remarried couples learn practical ways to give each other the royal treatment.

Rose is a popular speaker and a graduate of CLASS, Christian Leaders and Speakers Services. To have Rose speak to your group call (760) 346-9401 or write to her at 73-241 Highway 111, Suite 3D, Palm Desert, CA 92260.